Archives in the European Union

Report of the Group of Experts on the Coordination of Archives

EUROPEAN COMMISSION
Secretariat-General

Cataloguing data can be found at the end of this publication

Luxembourg: Office for Official Publications of the European Communities, 1994

ISBN 92-826-8233-1

Printed in Italy

FOREWORD

This report on European archives was requested by the Council of the European Communities and the Ministers for Culture of the Member States in a resolution they adopted jointly on 14 November 1991.[1] This date happens to fall midway between two important events: the fall of the Berlin Wall on 9 November 1989 and the entry into force of the Treaty on European Union (Maastricht Treaty) on 1 November 1993. What may be a pure coincidence is none the less highly significant and symbolic.

The fall of the Berlin Wall marked the end of the totalitarian regimes which continued to hold sway in Central and Eastern Europe after the downfall of the dictatorships which had ruled in the West in the first half of the 20th century. It was also the end of the ideologies which, with some exceptions, have so dominated the European continent throughout the century.

The Treaty on European Union recalls at once the historic importance of the ending of the division of the continent and the need to lay firm bases for the construction of the future Europe, by resolutely pursuing the process of creating an ever-closer union among the peoples of Europe and confirming the principles of liberty and democracy.

Coming between these two events, the resolution of 14 November 1991 stresses the role that the archival heritage will play in the Europe of the future as an indispensable instrument for writing the history of the whole continent or of the individual nations and as an aid to the functioning of democracy by offering both ordinary citizens and researchers easier access.

To achieve these two aims the resolution seeks to promote better structured and target-oriented forms of coordination and cooperation between the archive services of the Member States of the Community (now the Union) and between these services and the Union institutions. As stated in one of the chapters of the report, the archive work advocated by the resolution of 14 November 1991 is destined to transcend the geographical boundaries of the European Union and, like the Union itself, to extend to the entire continent.

The initiative of this report in the field of archives serves one of the objectives of the Treaty on European Union: to establish a citizenship common to nationals of the Member States, but it also inserts in its article G.37 that 'the Community shall contribute to the flowering of the cultures of the Member States, while respecting their national and regional diversity and at the same time bringing the common cultural heritage to the fore'.

---

[1] The full text of the resolution can be found at the beginning of the introduction to this report.

In laying the foundation stone for the European archives with a call directed in the first instance at the States of the Union, the resolution of 14 November 1991 invites the countries of Europe to read their history together and to find the source of a deep-rooted identity based on the values of liberty and democracy, which transcends but does not alter diversity.

This report has been produced by the heads of the Member States' archive services and other national experts, in close association with the European Commission. The other Community institutions and the European University Institute in Florence also collaborated. Its sole purpose is to make a contribution to the grand design of a free Europe, united by its history and the sharing of common democratic values.

Contents

INTRODUCTION

1. RESOLUTION OF 14 NOVEMBER 1991

On 14 November 1991 the Council and the Ministers for Culture meeting within the Council adopted a **resolution**[2] inviting the Commission:

(i) **to set up** a group of experts appointed on the proposal of the Member States, for the purpose of examining to what extent greater coordination of archives policy and practice within the Community is desirable;

(ii) **to transmit** a progress report by the group to the Council before the end of 1992.

A **progress report** was duly presented to the Council by the Commission on 23 November 1992[3] and the group's mandate extended for an extra six months because of the complex nature of the subject.

This **report** is the work of the group of national experts set up by the Commission in accordance with the resolution of 14 November 1991. The increasing overlapping of the public records of Member States and those of the Community, a state of affairs highlighted by the resolution, has led the Commission to seek the additional assistance of representatives of the institutions and of the European University Institute in Florence (EUIF), the repository of the Community's historical archives.

Some **30 national experts** and **representatives** of the institutions and the European University Institute in Florence (EUIF) took part in five meetings for the purposes of preparing the report; the meetings took place in Brussels on 31 March,

---

[2] The full text of the resolution, as published in the *Official Journal of the European Communities* (C 314, 5.12.1991, p. 2), is as follows:

'THE COUNCIL OF THE EUROPEAN COMMUNITIES AND THE MINISTERS FOR CULTURE MEETING WITHIN THE COUNCIL,
In view of the twofold role of archives as a basis for decision-making in the public sector on the one hand, and as a vital component of a nation's cultural heritage on the other;
In view of the increased intermingling of public records among Member States and between Member States and the Community, and bearing in mind the legislation concerning the opening to the public of the historical archives of the Community;
Bearing in mind that the European archival heritage provides an indispensable resource for writing the history of Europe or of an individual nation;
Considering that well-kept and accessible archives contribute greatly to the democratic functioning of our societies;
Considering that an adequate archives policy and efficient archives management create the conditions for the accessibility needed,
INVITE the Commission:
— to set up a group of experts appointed on the proposal of the Member States, for the purpose of examining to what extent greater coordination of archives policy and practice within the Community is desirable,
— to transmit a progress report by the group to the Council before the end of 1992'.
[3] SEC(92) 2092, 23.11.1992.

17 June and 24 September 1992 and 9 March and 23 April 1993.[4] A final meeting was held on 22 October 1993 to finalize the report with a view to publication. The list of experts and other representatives is at Annex 7 to this report.

Discussions mainly centred on the contributions from the Member States' experts (who were responsible for archives policy in their own countries). The Commission chaired the group and provided secretariat services.

2. 1983-1993

During these 10 years, a great deal has happened within the Community. The archives sector has been involved in the changes.

Since 1983 Community action has focused on opening the archives of the Community institutions[5] and a dialogue was initiated with the archive services of the Foreign Ministries.[6]

---

[4] *Belgium*: Ernest Persoons, Herman Coppens; *Denmark*: Johan Peter Noack, Michael H. Gelting; *Germany*: Friedrich P. Kahlenberg, Hans Schmitz, Hans-Joachim Schreckenbach; *Greece*: Marianna Kolyva, Nicolas Karapidakis; *Spain*: Margarita Vasquez de Parga; *France*: Jean Favier, François Renouard, Michel Duchein, Paule Rene-Bazin, Catherine Oudin; *Ireland*: David V. Craig, Patrick Buckley; *Italy*: Renato Grispo, Salvatore Mastruzzi, M. Pia Rinaldi Mariani, Paola Tascini Stella; *Luxembourg*: Cornel Meder; *Netherlands*: Eric Ketelaar; *Portugal*: Jorge Borges de Macedo, Manuela Mendonca; *United Kingdom*: Sarah Tyacke, Patrick Cadell; *European University Institute, Florence*: Jean-Marie Palayret; *Commission*: Lino Facco, Hans Hofmann, Jocelyne Collonval, René Brion, Jean-Louis Moreau; *Council*: Hartmut Berger; *European Parliament*: Jacques Schouller; *Court of Auditors*: Ian Hamilton; *Economic and Social Committee*: Costantino Picco; *Office for Official Publications of the European Communities*: John Young.

[5] The Regulation of 1 February 1983 and the Decision of 8 February 1983 opened to the public the historical archives of the ECSC, the EEC and Euratom (Council Regulation (EEC, Euratom) No 354/83 of 1 February 1983 and Commission Decision No 359/83/ECSC of 8 February 1983 (OJ L 43, 15.2.1983, pp. 1-3 and 14-15); reprinted in *Opening of the historical archives of the European Communities to the Public,* Office for Official Publications of the European Communities, Luxembourg, 1983, pp. 71-75.
This Regulation states that the Communities' historical archives will be opened after 30 years and also lays down a number of rules common to the Community and the Member States for handling these archives. The Directors of the National Archives of the Member States welcomed the 1983 measures in the following communiqué:
'The Directors of the National Archives of the Member States congratulate the European Communities on their decision to open their historical archives to the public in accordance with a 30-year rule, which is the access period in operation in the majority of the Member States. Through this decision, the European Communities are ensuring the preservation of their archival heritage and are making their historical archives available for research. With researchers turning their attention more and more to the study of contemporary history, this step by the European Communities will be greatly appreciated by historians, jurists, economists, political scientists and other users of archives. We are convinced that this Community initiative will lead to still closer cooperation between the archive services of the European Communities and those of the Member States' (op. cit., p. 77).

[6] *Guide to the archives of the Ministries of Foreign Affairs of the Member States of the European Communities and of the European Political Cooperation,* Office for Official Publications of the European Communities, Luxembourg, 1989. This 78-page guide is also available in the other eight official languages of the Community.

The Directors of the national archive services took various steps after 1989, mainly within the International Council on Archives, to arrange meetings to examine ways of improving coordination between the archival policies of the 12 Member States, including the Community archives in their investigations.

The meetings of the Directors of the national archive services led in particular to the proposal, which was presented to the Council of Ministers for Culture during the Dutch Presidency, that a group of experts, to be brought together by the Commission, should be given the task of examining the possibilities for coordination and cooperation over the entire range of the European archival heritage. This proposal resulted in the approval of the resolution of 14 November 1991. This resolution opens up a new area of work by giving the experts charge of an investigation which covers the field of archives in its entirety. This resolution opened up a wide field of research for the experts appointed; under their terms of reference, they were to examine to what extent greater coordination of archives policy and practice within the Community was desirable — a wide brief full of potential.

From the outset, the experts were aware of the danger of being isolated in a technical void instead of focusing on a specific cultural design and a plan to enhance democratic participation.

To achieve these objectives, the resolution lays stress on the need for a proper archives policy (and adequate resources) as well as effective archives management geared to increasing their accessibility.

However, it remains to be seen whether any form of bilateral, multilateral or Community cooperation can be worked out, where necessary, between the Member States to facilitate their task and enable them to share the not insignificant costs involved in carrying out certain kinds of work, especially that necessitating the use of modern technology.

3. TEN THEMES

The group's first step was to divide the subject up by theme. Some 40 documents and materials were assembled — mostly from the group's own resources — and the following themes identified:

(1)   Records management: appraisal and disposal
(2)   Physical conservation of archives
(3)   Practical conditions of access to archives
(4)   National legislation and access to archives
(5)   Management and storage of computerized archives (MRA)
(6)   Exchange of archival information and computer networks
(7)   Training of archivists and recognition of qualifications
(8)   Private archives
(9)   Community archives
(10) The Community and archives in Europe

Although this last theme did not strictly fall within the group's terms of reference, it was decided to devote an extra chapter to archives in the continent of Europe generally. It was felt that, in the interests of democracy and historical interpretation, proper use should be made of the European archival heritage, which means looking beyond the Community's present borders; after all, these are not fixed and are likely to be extended at some time or other. Even if resources are limited, the concept of the 'common house' is clearly relevant to European archives policy.

It was decided that the group would discuss each subject first to establish some guidelines before more detailed study was undertaken by an expert or experts with experience of the particular field. The whole group then met again at the end to approve the various papers and their conclusions. This report is, therefore, being presented as a collective effort.

Each chapter, however, has its own distinct character. Indeed, since the group was in agreement that papers should be practical and not be tied to a specific format, the conclusions vary in terms of their applicability and do not prejudge any decisions or measures that might be taken. In other words, the group has adopted an empirical approach and no attempt has been made to construct a system or theory.

4. STRUCTURE OF THE REPORT

In addition to this introduction, the report is presented in the following parts:

- Part One: a factual description of the present organization of Member States' archive services;
- Part Two: the chapters devoted to the 10 themes listed above (Section 3);
- Six technical annexes, plus a seventh annex listing all the experts involved in the group's work.

5. THE PARTS AND CHAPTERS IN BRIEF

What follows is in no way a summary. The aim instead is to give a brief outline of the contents and themes covered.

Part One: The present organization of archives in the Member States

This first part gives an overview of national archive services in the Member States from an organizational standpoint. For a number of reasons, public records in the Member States are organized in different ways, in terms both of structure and of function. Before any new measures are taken in a Community context, it is important to have a clear picture of the current situation, based on the information available, before taking appropriate action.

Part Two: Themes for coordination and cooperation

Chapter 1 — Records management: appraisal and disposal

There has been such an explosion in the quantity of documents that it is not possible to conserve everything. On the other hand, the destruction of a series of documents, or even just one document, may constitute an irreparable loss for the history of a country, a region or a period. Records review has therefore become an important subject, although there are no absolute rules as yet. Civil services and national archive services need to cooperate actively, with the latter being brought in to help with reviewing operations; 'pre-archive' deposits could prove useful here. Selection methods should be coordinated at national level, and exchanges of information and experience between Member States organized to help improve them. This might in the end lead to a review model that could be used both nationally and at European level and which would provide a valuable point of reference in such a sensitive area.

Chapter 2 — The material preservation of archives

The physical conservation of documents is one of the main duties of the archivist. If this role is to be fulfilled, there need to be enough suitably equipped buildings. Member States and the Community institutions would do well to acquaint them-selves with current quality standards in this area with a view to using them as a basis for construction or renovation projects. Attention also needs to be paid to the type of equipment to be used (shelves, containers, etc.), since not all products available on the market are suitable. As was the case with research into permanent paper, cooperation between Member States is particularly worthwhile when the cost of modern conservation technology is especially high, an important factor given the growing volume of audiovisual and computer archives. In addition, if archives are threatened or damaged by a disaster of some kind, international financial assistance, particularly the Community's, needs to be available to pre-vent, limit or repair the damage. Expenditure should be covered by the emergency assistance the Community grants in such cases.

Chapter 3 — The practical conditions of access to archives

National archives should be doing all they can to facilitate user access. To the extent permitted by financial resources and the requirements of preservation, they should provide users with the best possible facilities for consulting archives (properly equipped reading rooms, opening hours, copying facilities, etc.). These are tasks which all Member States should be tackling together if the policy announced in the resolution of 14 November 1991 of opening up the archives to as many users as possible, ordinary citizens as well as researchers, is to be successful. The rules should ensure that access formalities are not too complex and do not discriminate against non-nationals, and should not impose unduly heavy charges. In terms of the practical conditions of access, the Member States should be cooperating with each other to draft, disseminate and where necessary translate appropriate finding aids.

Chapter 4 — National legislation and access to archives

The 30-year rule for opening historical archives to the public is now standard in all Member States. This should be seen as more of an upper limit than a lower limit, and in some quarters it is thought it should be lowered in keeping with present feeling about freedom of information. However, Member States have created a number of legal exceptions and in the interests of transparency these need to be better known by researchers and other archive users. Coordination to be considered here might involve looking at ways of harmonizing these exceptions, perhaps in the form of an agreement.

Chapter 5 — The management and storage of computerized archives

This is an important area on account of the growing use of computers by public services and the resulting proliferation of data that has been produced, modified, exchanged and preserved using this medium — the so-called paperless environment. There is a danger of computerized data losing its identity during the course of its administrative 'life' or, in the case of personal information, of being prematurely destroyed. As far as historical archives are concerned, the equipment or software used for storing data may have become obsolete, making consultation more difficult. If there is to be sufficient continuity in processing, National Archives need to be involved from the beginning in setting up computerized archives, as indeed is already the case in some Member States. There is plenty of scope here for cooperation on a joint research programme to develop a general computerized archive management and storage model.

Chapter 6 — The exchange of archival information and computer networks between the Member States

The new information technologies can provide speedier, more effective and decentralized access to information. In contrast to other information sectors, however, National Archives have fallen some way behind in this area. There are a number of reasons why this situation should have arisen. Even at national level, relatively little has been achieved. In addition, those projects which have been carried out had to use whatever standards were available in the absence of standards specifically relating to archives. Until such time as there is progress toward setting up a European network for archival information exchange, there is a need for intermediate initiatives such as: an inventory of computer applications in use in the Member States, with their potential for archival information exchange; the development of special archive standards and, in the interim, the selection and dissemination of standards that come closest to meeting archival principles; the creation of databases using descriptive standards agreed by all.

Chapter 7 — The training of archivists and recognition of diplomas

Training for archivists has radically changed since the Second World War and especially during the last 10 years. These changes have also affected the archivist's professional image, largely because of the increased use of modern information-processing techniques. At the same time, however, the archivist still plays the key role in organizing and exploiting archives. The role has also widened, to such an extent that training programmes for archivists have already had to be revised in several Member States in order to keep abreast of changing requirements.

Training is available at various levels, all of which would gain were the profession of archivist to be officially recognized by the Member States. Indeed, such recognition is an essential prerequisite for the mutual recognition of qualifications. Archivists need to adopt a higher profile; their role is, after all, to safeguard a heritage which is a fount of regional or national identity and democratic ideals.

Nowadays, archivists have to acquire and develop skills in a number of different areas such as computers, information science, history and languages.

Training for archivists cannot take place in isolation — it has to move with the times. There should be scope for exchanges and ongoing activities. The Community could contribute by encouraging archivists to take part in programmes such as Erasmus, Tempus or Lingua.

Chapter 8 — Private archives

Private archives are an important part of the archival heritage. By their very nature they may change location or even be destroyed, which could mean a country or a region losing an important body of historical or cultural information. However, there are marked differences in the steps Member States have taken to safeguard them, with some countries not having taken any measures at all. This is another area ripe for cooperation within a Community framework, especially as the opening-up of the single market may give rise to abuses. Since January 1993 a regulation and a directive on the movement of cultural goods have come into force, archives being covered providing they are more than 50 years old. However, Member State administrations need to cooperate properly if the regulations are to be effective. There is considerable scope for cooperation between Member States for the purposes of safeguarding and exploiting private archives in conjunction with their owners.

Chapter 9 — The Community archives

In 1983, following an agreement between the Member States and the institutions, two legal texts were adopted by the Council and the Commission to open up the Community archives to the public under the 30-year rule. Further cooperation in this field led to the publication of a guide to the archives of the Ministries of Foreign Affairs and the Community institutions. In addition, the latter agreed to deposit the originals of public archives with the European University Institute in Florence. The chapter also describes how the institutions have cooperated among themselves as well as with Member States and national archivists' associations.

Chapter 10 — The Community and archives in Europe

The 1991 resolution highlights the importance of the European archival heritage for the writing of the history of Europe. The concept of a European archival heritage should in fact be extended to the whole continent because, whether countries are inside or outside the Community, they have much of their history in common. The Community is, after all, not a fixed and closed entity. It started with six members and now has 12 and further enlargement is likely. By cooperating in the safeguarding and exploitation of archives beyond the Community's present frontiers, the Community would be doing history a service and helping to strengthen democracy in Europe.

6. PRINCIPAL FINAL CONCLUSIONS

6.1. Follow-up to the resolution of 14 November 1991

The resolution of 14 November 1991 highlights the European significance of Member States' archival heritage, reflecting the fact that for the last 40 years they have been partners in the process of European integration. The resolution seeks to encourage closer cooperation between national archive services so they can play their part in historical research and the democratic functioning of Europe.

The group is aware that this report does not deal exhaustively with the main issue raised by the resolution of 14 November 1991: namely, the identification of all the potential areas for cooperation and, where appropriate, coordination between the Member States and the Community institutions.

The group has attempted to identify a certain number of areas in which efforts should be concentrated and to come up with ways of organizing joint action and research.

6.2. Proposals for joint action and research

The group is convinced that for the time being the best way of obtaining coordination in archival matters is to develop and promote active cooperation, on the basis of mutual agreement rather than regulation, whether at Community or extra-Community level.

Thus Member States will be able to develop cooperation between their archive services, taking advantage, where appropriate, of the possibilities offered by the Community, but always respecting the principle of subsidiarity.

In practice in the field of archives there are technical matters which are on such a scale that a pooling of research and resources is essential. Besides, for matters which relate to culture and tradition, no quick decision can be made as to the best solution for the problems raised in this report.

Having completed its work on the subjects which were set before it, the group considered that the following actions could be undertaken. They are listed in an order of priority which is both indicative and practical.

6.2.1. Movement of cultural goods — Administrative cooperation in the archive field

With the advent of the single market, a number of measures have been taken at Community level to regulate the export of cultural goods. Provision has been made for setting up an appropriate system of authorization, and the need for clearly defined measures in terms of both their scope and their application has been recognized. In view of the cultural specificity of archives, national archive services should be requested to prepare a special administrative protocol on archives in cooperation with the Commission and with the committee set up under Council Regulation (EEC) No 3911/92 of 9 December 1992.[7]

Steps need to be taken to counteract any problems that the free movement of goods may cause for archives. In particular, Member States, with the support of the Community, should take action to develop a European network of information on the movement of archive material.

6.2.2. Physical and material conservation of archives

Keeping archives in good condition, whatever the medium, is one of the main tasks of national archive services. The job is not always easy and can be expensive. In any event, it is something for which the authorities are directly responsible.

(a) *Quality of buildings*

Standards for buildings and their facilities should be more widely known and observed at Community level. They can be used as references in construction or renovation projects.

(b) *Computerized archives (MRA)*

The continued expansion of computerized archives poses problems which have not been encountered before. As was the case for permanent paper, research is urgently needed to help Member States arrive at a common definition of physical conservation standards for this new type of archive and to develop an appropriate management model that draws on all that has been learned in this area.

(c) *Emergency aid in the event of disasters*

Whatever precautions are taken, archives are still at risk from disasters of natural or criminal origin. In the event of one occurring, Member States should be able to count on the Community's support to meet the cost of limiting or repairing the damage caused.

Member States and the institutions should be asked on what conditions archives should be eligible for emergency aid from the Community in the event of imminent

---

[7] Council Regulation (EEC) No 3911/92 of 9 December 1992 on the export of cultural goods (OJ L 395, 31.12.1993, pp. 1-3). See also Commission Regulation (EEC) No 752/93 of 30 March 1993 laying down provisions for the implementation of Council Regulation (EEC) No 3911/92 on the export of cultural goods (OJ L 77, 31.3.1993, pp. 24-26).

or sudden disaster. Given that archives are an irreplaceable cultural heritage, such a procedure, the rules of which have yet to be decided, is fully justified.

6.2.3. Records management: appraisal and disposal

Care should be exercised when destroying documents or files on the grounds that they are not of immediate interest to the departments that produced them, or they take up room which is needed for other purposes; they may be of relevance to future generations or historians. Even if it is not possible to keep everything, the opinion of archivists should be sought and they should be involved in any review procedure to ensure that nothing crucial is discarded. Even if there are no hard and fast rules, it is not enough to proceed on an *ad hoc* basis — some form of organization based on standard criteria is required.

A system needs to be set up for the exchange of experience and information between Member States with the involvement of the Community institutions. Such an exchange would be extremely useful, and could eventually lead to the establishment of records management schedules which could be used as examples of best practice for different national or regional administrations.

6.2.4. Access to archives: problems

If archives are to be of use to all potential users, which was one of the intentions of the resolution of 14 November 1991, access to them should not only be made easier but also standardized in all Member States in accordance with fair and liberal criteria. Archival information should also make use of modern computer resources and telecommunications technology for long-distance dissemination purposes.

In the Community context, this means that:

(1) exceptions to the 30-year rule, which is enforced in all Member States, should be identified and attempts made to establish where convergence might be appropriate, with due allowance for the need to safeguard privacy and State interests;

(2) at a practical level, all users of archives should be treated equally and should be allowed to move freely within the Community;

(3) the use of computer technology in archive management and utilization should be encouraged by drawing on experts to help frame, at Community level, appropriate descriptive standards, and the Commission should be requested to include this in its programme of action.

6.2.5. Training and mutual recognition of diplomas

The profession of archivist is changing and expanding to respond to the increased tasks expected of it. Training, therefore, needs to reflect these new requirements and adapt accordingly. Archivists nowadays need to be highly qualified, and their role should be properly recognized.

The group therefore considers that, with the prospect of mutual recognition of archive diplomas by Member States, it would be advisable as a first step to coordinate training programmes, to encourage collaboration between archive schools, and to enable persons involved to benefit from interuniversity exchanges such as those set up by Erasmus, Lingua, etc.

Studies, however, are not enough; archivists should be encouraged to move between Member States to continue their training, and specialist seminars should be organized at Community level.

6.2.6. Private archives and initiatives by associations and research centres

Given the importance of private archives from the point of view of the archival heritage, the group would like to see the administrative cooperation discussed at point 6.2.1 extended to this sector. There needs to be consultation with owners, custodians and donors of private archives to ensure that these valuable resources are properly cared for and not unlawfully exported outside the Community.

In addition, certain measures should be taken by Member States in favour of owners or custodians of archives, so as to encourage them to preserve and develop their heritage.

In this context it is worth mentioning the useful assistance which can be given by societies and research foundations which act in each Member State to encourage the preservation and exploitation of private archives.

7. STARTING WORK ON THE EUROPEAN ARCHIVES

The proposals made in Section 6 above are only the visible tip of a vast venture outlined in this report.

This venture, launched by the resolution of 14 November 1991, is the creation of the European archives, to be opened as we are about to enter the 21st century.

Now that the principal materials have been brought together, the Member States are ready to embark on this major task with the assistance of the Community institutions.

The aim is not only to preserve Europe's archival heritage, but also to make it an instrument for writing history and a means of actively serving democracy and the functioning of democracy.

The venture concerns the entire continent of Europe, which shares a common history and which, in the course of this century, has freed itself from the grips of many dictators.

This revival of archival work based on cooperation across frontiers will be an important contribution to the definition and assertion of the European identity.

Part One

THE PRESENT ORGANIZATION
OF ARCHIVES
IN THE MEMBER STATES

NATIONAL ARCHIVE SERVICES

The first part of this report is concerned with describing the institutional framework of the various Member States. This results from a long historical development peculiar to each one of them.

Without wishing to seek legislative or statutory harmonization, it seemed of interest to begin a report which could lead to joint projects being organized within the Community with a description of the existing situation within the various Member States.

The National Archives of the 12 Member States, which on the face of it play a similar role in each State, have in fact been given markedly different roles. For example, their jurisdiction does not extend indiscriminately to all national administrative bodies. Similarly, apart from the fact that some States have a centralized and some a decentralized administration, the National Archives have varied responsibilities with regard to the archives of the local authorities. Moreover, these same National Archives are involved in varying degrees in the organization of current and medium-term archives (still under the responsibility of the sectors which produced them). In this respect, the protection of national archival heritage, which is one of the main functions of the National Archives, can be facilitated by continuous or intermittent inspection within the authorities.

However, regardless of the differences between the functions of the National Archives, it should not be forgotten that archives are increasingly — and everywhere — proving to be a key factor in the cultural purposes of the Member States and of the Community.

1. A STATE DEPARTMENT

Any exchange between the various Member States relating to various archival matters depends on a good knowledge of national situations which are, in many respects, very diverse. The fundamental roles of the National Archives are to protect national archival heritage and to make this heritage available to all citizens. Having been organized in very different eras, modern National Archives come under different supervisory authorities:

BELGIUM	The Ministry of Scientific Policy
DENMARK	The Ministry of Cultural Affairs
GERMANY (Bundesarchiv)	The Ministry of the Interior
GREECE	The Ministry of National Education and Religion
SPAIN	The Ministry of Culture
FRANCE	The Ministry of National Education and Culture
IRELAND	Minister for Arts, Culture and the Gaeltacht. The Taoiseach (Prime Minister) remains responsible for matters concerning access
ITALY	The Ministry of Cultural and Environmental Goods
LUXEMBOURG	The Ministry of Cultural Affairs
NETHERLANDS	The Ministry of Welfare, Health and Cultural Affairs
PORTUGAL	The President of the Council of Ministers
UNITED KINGDOM (PRO)	The Lord Chancellor

There are historical reasons for these links with such-and-such a supervisory Ministry.

The case of Germany reflects, with regard to its *Länder*, the diversity of the European positions. Supervision of the archives is the responsibility, according to the case, of the Ministry of Cultural Affairs, of Sciences and Arts, of Public Education, even of the State Chancellery or the Senate.

The State Chancellery	Hamburg, Lower-Saxony, Saarland
Culture/Sciences and Arts	Baden-Württemberg, Bavaria, Berlin, Brandenburg, Bremen, Hesse, Mecklenburg-Western Pomerania, North Rhine-Westphalia, Rhineland-Palatinate, Schleswig-Holstein, Thuringia
Interior	Saxony, Saxony-Anhalt

Finally, in the United Kingdom, the archives service is responsible to various ministries, according to where they are situated:

• in England and Wales: the PRO (Public Record Office), in London, comes under the Lord Chancellor's Department;

4

- in Scotland: the SRO (Scottish Record Office), in Edinburgh, comes under the Scottish Office;
- in Northern Ireland: the PRO (Public Record Office), in Belfast, comes under the Department of the Environment of the Northern Ireland Office.

In eight Member States of the Community (Belgium, France, Greece, Ireland, Italy, the Netherlands, Portugal, the United Kingdom), the minister responsible can rely on the work of an Archives Advisory Committee, upon which sit archivists and often representatives of the public services and the government, along with technical experts. These advisory committees do not all have the same jurisdiction (see Annex 2).

2. THE DIVERSITY OF FUNCTIONS OF THE NATIONAL ARCHIVES[8]

The activities of the National Archives vary from one Member State to another. This is basically a question of:

(a) historical tradition; thus 'records management' or management of current and medium-term archives is (still) not everywhere given as one of the functions of the National Archives;

(b) human resources and financial means; available funding with regard to buildings and personnel for the National Archives is very variable;

(c) legal framework; certain Member States do not have the necessary legal framework for developing their activities as could be desired.

In total, the functions for which the National Archives of the 12 Member States are responsible vary markedly, whether considering their responsibilities with regard to central government archives, regional or local government archives, or current and medium-term archives. These three aspects of their responsibility will now be examined.

2.1. Central government archives

In each Member State, the National Archives' principal duty is to look after the country's central government archives. However, not all central government departments necessarily come under the jurisdiction of the National Archives: some departments have their own archive organization, with regard to both current and historical archives.

---

[8] Concerning European Community archives, see Chapter 9.

Governmental bodies at a national or federal level which are free of the jurisdiction of the National Archives

Member State	Foreign affairs	Defence	Parliament	Public bodies	Various
BELGIUM	Yes	Yes	Yes[9]	Optional	
DENMARK	No[10]	No	Yes	Radio and Television: No	
GERMANY	No	No[11]	Yes	No	Federal Reserve Bank: No
GREECE	Yes	Yes	Yes		
SPAIN	Yes	Yes	Yes		Council of State: Yes[12]
FRANCE	Yes	Yes	No	No	Council of State: No
IRELAND	No	Yes[13]	Yes		
ITALY	Yes	Yes[14]		Yes	
LUXEMBOURG	No				
NETHER-LANDS	No	No	No	No	
PORTUGAL	Yes	Yes	Yes		Other ministries: Yes
UNITED KINGDOM	No	No	Yes	Mostly: No	Radio and Television: Yes

Yes: Free from jurisdiction by the National Archives.
No: Under the jurisdiction of the National Archives.

---

[9] The Belgian Parliament has already placed archives with the National Archives, although it is not obliged to do so.

[10] Archives prior to 1945 have been placed with the National Archives.

[11] The Ministry of Defence is served by a specific division of the Bundesarchiv.

[12] In Spain, the Ministry of Defence, the National Heritage, the public universities, the Council for Scientific Research, the Spanish Institute, the Royal Academies, the Royal Place and the Courts can themselves carry out preservation of their medium-term and historical archives. In spite of this, they can take advantage, if they wish, of the services of the State Archives and place their medium-term and historical archives in the latter's repositories. These archives are not administered directly by the Ministry of Culture, but since the State is the holder, all prescriptive machinery emanating from the Ministry of Culture, which is the competent department with regard to archives (Law of Spanish Historical Heritage, Archives Regulation, etc.) comes under its authority.

[13] The National Archives Act also applies to the archives of the Ministry of Defence, but these are kept in a separate military repository.

[14] Civil archives are distinguished from military archives; only the latter are classified, and the National Archives have jurisdiction over the civil archives of the Ministry of Defence.

2.2. Regional or local government archives

The administrative structure of the Member States is reflected in the organization of their archival networks, which may be centralized or decentralized.

Belgium, Denmark, Greece, France, Italy, the Netherlands and Portugal could belong to a first group: in these countries, regional government archives are responsible in several respects to a central archival authority having jurisdiction over the whole country. In Italy, and to some extent in France, Belgium and Denmark, local government archives are also responsible to the central archival authority. [15]

In Italy, municipal, provincial and regional councils are obliged to provide a separate service for their archives which date back more than 40 years, even though the National Archives exercise control over them. The 20 superintendents responsible for inspecting the archives must approve decisions by the municipalities relating to the disposal of documents.

Germany, as a Federal Republic, is a specific case: a central administration of archives does not exist at Republic level. The Bundesarchiv has jurisdiction only over archives produced by the Federal Government. The archives of regional bodies are kept by the archive services of the *Länder*. As with all cultural policy, archival questions come under the jurisdiction of the *Länder*. Each *Land* has its own archival organization. Certain interests in common between the various *Länder* and the Federal Government are discussed in the Konferenz der Archivreferenten (Archive Advisors' Conference). Local archives come under the archival legislation of the *Länder*. The archives of regional bodies of the Federal State are preserved by the archive services of the *Länder*.

In the United Kingdom, the Public Record Office (PRO) in London has jurisdiction over central government archives in England and Wales. The local authorities have their own archive repositories, regional and local, independent of administration by the Public Record Office. The Scottish Record Office (SRO) in Edinburgh and the Public Record Office (PRO) in Belfast have jurisdiction over the archives of the central governments of Scotland and Northern Ireland respectively. In Scotland, local government districts are served by independent archival services. In Northern Ireland, the PRO in Belfast has jurisdiction over local and provincial archives.

In Belgium, Denmark, the Netherlands, Italy and Portugal, the National Archives have decentralized regional archive repositories. Archives relating to the region

---

[15] At the third European Conference on Archives, held in Vienna from 11 to 15 May 1993, which was initiated by the International Council on Archives, emphasis was placed on the importance of the regions not only from an economic point of view but also culturally. This importance is particularly obvious with regard to trans-frontier regions or zones, in which specialized forms of cooperation have arisen through economic development centres. Following upon this, new organizational and legal structures have authority to cover operations taking place on both sides of the frontiers at the same time. Such developments will also have repercussions with regard to archives.

Care should be taken that this dispersal of archive producers, separated by a frontier, does not lead to risks of the loss or disappearance of archives. Such archives would, without doubt, be better supervised amicably at a Community level.

where the repository is situated are in the main stored there and, if necessary, central government archives which emanate from the province. In Italy, in addition, regional repositories established in the main provincial towns have, if necessary, additional archive repositories in the small towns when it is considered preferable to preserve the archives *in situ*.

In Spain, there is also a tendency to grant greater autonomy regarding the archival heritage to the 17 recognized Autonomous Communities. The National Archives (administration of State archives by the Ministry of Culture) remain responsible for the management of medium-term and historical archives produced by the central government. But the management of almost all the repositories named 'Provincial historical archives' where the archives of the provincial bodies are placed, together with those of the courts which do not have national jurisdiction and those of solicitors, etc., is at present the responsibility of the Autonomous Communities. As far as the local authorities are concerned, these have a level of autonomy in managing their archives, even though the law on archives also applies to them.

In the Netherlands, where the local authorities have their own archive repositories, managed by the local secretary or by a professional archivist, several of these have grouped together in order to preserve their archives at a shared cost; archives from the central State are preserved in the repositories thus established.

In England and also Scotland, the county archives can be given documents produced by the departments of the central government, but it is a matter of specific agreements. The UK National Archives only inspect county archives in so far as these repositories preserve archives from the central State. In England, 20% of definitive public archives from central government are preserved outside the PRO in repositories approved by the latter. In France, the regions do not have their own repositories at present and in general place their archives within departmental repositories. In Ireland local archive services exist solely in the cities and the counties of Dublin, Cork and Limerick.

There is no similar repository in the other 23 counties.

2.3. Current and semi-current (intermediate) archives

Whilst all the National Archives are responsible for the processing and preservation of historical archives, the control which they exercise over current and semi-current archives is more or less extensive as the case may be.

Each Member State has formulated original ways of coordinating the work of the archive-producing departments with that of the National Archives. Most Member States exercise a level of control over archives throughout their life cycle. But the idea of control varies from one Member State to another, this being related to their historical traditions. During the last 20 years most of the Member States have made significant progress in this area, often expressed through legal changes.

The National Archives of Spain and France, the PRO in London and the German Bundesarchiv manage semi-current records centres. The National Archives of Denmark, Spain, Italy, the Netherlands, Portugal and the United Kingdom and the German Bundesarchiv make listings of semi-current archives. The Law expressly gives responsibility for this task to the National Archives in Denmark and the Netherlands. In nearly all the Member States, the National Archives supply technical assistance to authorities which request it and are also involved in the development of standard management approaches (methods, standards, rules) and in that of classification systems. The National Archives are almost everywhere involved in training personnel from the authorities and from semi-current archive repositories.

Amongst the systems adopted for inspection of the archives of the various authorities, the National Archives of several Member States carry out occasional visits.

The National Archives' responsibilities and right to inspect with regard to sorting and disposal are examined in Chapter 1 of Part Two.

Some factual data concerning the present situation with regard to the management of current and semi-current archives in various Member States is given below.

BELGIUM

The National Archives have regular contact with the various government departments. Since 1988, the National Archives have updated the classification schemes for archives produced by central government.

DENMARK

A Ministerial Order of 1992 (replacing the 1976 Order) organized systematic collaboration between the authorities and the National Archives. Since around 1950, the National Archives and Municipal Archives have assisted the authorities in managing current archives from the time they are created. Essential documents are protected from the time they are created. The national archivist authorizes any disposal of central government archives.

GERMANY

The Bundesarchiv has a consultative voice regarding the management of current archives. It is responsible for managing semi-current archives (Zwischenarchiv).

GREECE

The National Archives inspect the authorities' semi-current repositories. The managers of the provincial archive repositories inspect the semi-current archives in their areas.

SPAIN

Since 1969 there have been communal semi-current archive repositories for the central authorities. These semi-current repositories are managed by the State Archives.

Since 1985, a mixed committee (archive-producing authorities and the State Archives) has been in charge of the description and assessment of documents. This assessment of the value of each set of archive documents has consequences regarding the choice of the place of transfer, the possible decision to dispose of the set and also the system of subsequent access.

The State Archives inspect the archives of public bodies.

FRANCE

The inspection of central government current and semi-current archives is carried out by the National Archives over the whole country. Permanent or temporary assignments by State archivists in the central authorities have existed since 1952. The managers of the departmental archives inspect the current and semi-current archives of the regional authorities.

IRELAND

Each ministry has an official responsible for contacts with the National Archives.

ITALY

The jurisdiction of the National Archives extends to the current archives of governmental bodies, both on a national and local level. Mixed supervisory committees of State archivists and government officials exist on a national and provincial level. They carry out a right of inspection and inventory. They supervise the review, preservation, classification, description and possible advance opening of the archives.

NETHERLANDS

The supervision of current and semi-current archives produced by the central government comes under the National Archives (inspection, management assistance, classification and inventory of current and semi-current archives, drawing up schedules of disposable items, developing automation programmes, etc.) with occasional advice from the Archives Board (advice on schedules of disposable items). Pre-archive centres exist which are managed by certain archive-producing authorities.

The authorities must classify and inventory archives before they are deposited, in accordance with standards which have been determined by the National Archives.

PORTUGAL

The National Archives give technical assistance to all State institutions and departments. They are responsible for introducing general technical directives for the organization of semi-current archives and for determining which archives from the State, the local authorities and the public authorities are to be classified as national archival heritage.

UNITED KINGDOM

The Public Record Office (PRO), in Kew, London, coordinates and supervises the review and preservation of archives which come under its jurisdiction. Permanent assignments of State archivists to the authorities are envisaged. Each ministry has an official responsible for contact with the PRO. The PRO has organized a vast centre for review and semi-current deposit in Hayes (Middlesex) where, however, the maintenance of the archives comes under the responsibility of the archive-producing departments. In Edinburgh, the personnel of the Scottish Record Office (SRO) supervises the management of archives produced by the departments of the Scottish Office.

Part Two

THEMES FOR COORDINATION
AND COOPERATION

CHAPTER 1

RECORDS MANAGEMENT: APPRAISAL AND DISPOSAL

Although the problem has become immediate as a result of the huge increase in the mass of documentation produced by the public authorities, there is not at the present time an absolute or even a dominant method of appraisal and disposal of documents and records. This is a dilemma, since while it is not possible to preserve everything, the destruction of a document can represent an irreparable loss for the future. However, regulations and practices exist in the Member States which at least confront the problem, in spite of their seeming inadequacy in the face of a situation which is becoming more and more complex. A comparison of these regulations and practices could prove to be extremely useful in improving the methodology of selection by means of reciprocal contributions and ensuring continuous improvement based on a range of national experience.

Appraisal and disposal has to be very arbitrary, taking into account the different interests which are at stake. Since the authorities, for their part, are concerned with immediate and administrative matters, archivists are called upon to play the role of intermediary between the archive-producing authorities on the one hand and the world of research and the general public on the other. In the end it is a question of encouraging continuity between the creators, the managers and the preservers of archives, by organizing direct collaboration between them within an officially affirmed and established organizational structure. The National Archives must be able to participate actively and as quickly as possible in the inspection of disposal, by government departments, of those archives which they no longer need in their operation. It is also necessary to shorten the distance between current archives and historical archives by establishing, if necessary, pre-archive repositories within which selection could be carried out as wished, by combining the knowledge which government departments have of their files and the preoccupations of the archivists who inherit them.

With regard to both organizational questions and selection criteria, a pooling of information and experience should allow for the creation of a model on a national and possibly European level which could serve as a reference for appraisal and disposal of documents and records.

1.1. THE PROBLEM

From the beginning of the 20 th century, the problem of the quantity of documents produced by government departments has been of concern to nearly all European countries. Since that time the problem has continued to grow: the written document remains one of the main methods used for transmitting and confirming information between citizens and those who govern them.

In spite of the progress made in information technology, the development of audiovisual equipment and the increased use of new media, nearly all official documents are still written in black on white. In fact, the speed of production of written administrative archives is increasing daily in accordance with the multiplication of State departments, in spite of the boom in new technology. Moreover, the problem of appraisal and disposal also relates to archives preserved on the new media.

Alongside the growth in the mass of documents produced, the archive services are faced with a growth in their 'customers': the era during which only historians were interested in the information preserved in the archives is in the past. Today, the archives' customers are not limited to individual researchers but have broadened to include every citizen.

The documents which are researched by the users often have very diverse origins and are, as a consequence, widely dispersed. They also show a wide diversity of viewpoint: for present research and still more for that of the future, there are no insignificant documents, hence no more harmless destruction. The resulting problem, which is of concern to archivists throughout the world — can be summed up as follows:

(a) the mass of documents — a potential source of information — is multiplying daily;

(b) the needs of the users (departments, researchers) are constantly expanding;

(c) it is impossible to preserve everything;

(d) it is impossible to sort the archives document by document.

1.2. REVIEW METHODS

In spite of the difficulties caused by the contingencies of everyday life, which have no time for certain theoretical archival ideas, it is imperative to try at least to retain control of the archives produced by the authorities in the course of their activities.

Known methods, (review, statistical sampling, representative sampling, random sampling, etc.) seem to be unfortunately inadequate to the need. They do, however, attempt to follow the development of need in order to protect as much information as possible for researchers of the future.

This is therefore a point upon which convergence can be researched at Community level.

1.3. RECOMMENDATIONS FOR COORDINATION

There is no standard method for the selection of various types of archival documents. With regard to appraisal and disposal there are differences in methods and procedures from one Member State to another, in addition to differences in responsibilities of archive-producing departments. The differences in methods concern the circuitous routes for disposal requests, the definition of authority with regard to review schedules, the degree of authority which archivists hold in these operations, their degree of responsibility, the role of the various departments (archive-producing departments, pre-archives, historical archives) (see Annex 3).

Moreover, the development of research and the expansion in consultation needs do not make things easier: the archivist of today is obliged to anticipate the preoccupations of the researchers of tomorrow, using yesterday's requests and remaining attentive to the research tendencies of today.

In any event, it is imperative that appraisal and disposal should be organized through collaboration between the National Archives and the archive-producing departments. The usefulness of this collaboration is based on two observations: the archive-producing departments unquestionably recognize the administrative and legal significance of the documents which they produced or receive; they are also in a position to explain the relationships between their files and those of other departments; on the other hand, archivists, as a result of their training, their experience and the contacts which they have with the users of archives, are qualified to single out those documents which contain information which is of use to research in general. In future, in nearly all the Member States, no destruction of archives produced by the public authorities will take place without authorization from the National Archives.

Ideally, the National Archives must be able to supervise and inspect the review of archives before the disposal of those which the government no longer needs in its daily operations.

Firstly there is good reason for developing the criteria of appraisal and disposal at national level, including guidance schedules, taking into account the work in progress by national groups which are specialized in this area. A European working party, composed of experts in the field, would then be more capable of preparing a manual for the management of public sector archives, which would be valuable for the government departments of the Member States.

Similarly, personnel from the archive-producing departments and from the National Archives would have to be closely associated during review operations, regardless of the importance of the government department in question.

Moreover, the adoption of appropriate measures moving in this direction — taking into account the specific requirements of each Member State — would gradually release qualified archive personnel from very onerous tasks. It would be an advantage to have a large part of the work already carried out before the arrival of the archives at the repository, by specially trained personnel from the archive-producing department under the supervision of personnel from the National Archives.

Regular placing in medium-term repositories would allow continuity in archival work and would disencumber the authorities and the historical archive repositories.

In this same connection, in order to simplify repetitive procedures and obtain a better use of time — thus allowing the possibility of more intensive work on the problem of selection of archives — two other projects could be envisaged:

(i) computerization of all the national archives and familiarization of personnel with data processing on a daily basis (the programmes becoming more and more accessible to those not specialized in computers);

(ii) the development (by a group of archivists and computer experts) of programmes specially designed for the management of archival sorting, adapted to archival principles.

There is no doubt that use of the Member States' experience of review procedures will be critical in order to avoid the loss of important archives. This experience, assisted by a systematic use of data processing, will be a decisive factor regarding the optimum use of the information produced and preserved in the form of archives.

By taking advantage of the advice of experts knowing the practices of the various Member States with regard to records management, it should be possible to attempt a model of 'progressive review schedules', limiting this at first to a certain number of types of collection which exist in most Member States (which do not necessitate a long archival-legal analysis). This would develop towards a harmonization of review and preservation periods and later towards the production of a records management manual for public sector archives which would be valuable for all similar departments in the various Member States.

CHAPTER 2

THE MATERIAL PRESERVATION OF ARCHIVES

The material conditions of preservation are of major concern to administrators of the National Archives in the Member States.

Firstly, the question of buildings is often particularly acute, not only because the National Archives suffer from a chronic lack of space but sometimes also because of the pitiful state of some working premises and repositories.

There is also the question of the compliance of numerous buildings and their suitability with regard to the specific safety standards required for the preservation and use of archives recorded on paper and at present also those of archives on new media (audiovisual archives, for example).

Although less of a priority, the question also relates to storage equipment (shelves and archive boxes, etc.) in general because of the variety and poor quality of certain material offered on the market and more particularly because of the quality of the paper used, as a result of the tendency of present components to deteriorate.

With regard to archive buildings, it seems difficult at present to carry out forms of real collaboration between the Member States. On the other hand, through an appropriate declaration, the Council and the Ministers for Culture could jointly confirm the importance of the problem and remind the authorities and operators of the existing standards of excellence, which should in as far as possible be applied to building, renovation and adaptation projects relating to archive buildings.

On the other hand, full collaboration between the Member States is justified when the costs incurred by modern processing or new preservation technology prove to be particularly high. This is the case, for example:

(i) in the field of permanent and copying paper for documents, used either for security copies or with a view to exchanges;

(ii) in researching mass deacidification;

(iii) in the equipment necessary for preserving audiovisual or computerized archives.

Finally, in the case where the archival heritage may be gravely threatened or damaged through disaster, its protection or salvaging should benefit

17

from assistance on an international level and particularly from the Community through urgent aid.

Archivists have, over the years, given considerable thought to the subjects raised in this chapter, and much has been written about all of them. It has therefore been considered wise to touch on the main problems, and on possible areas of cooperation, and then to refer to the existing literature, some of which is looked upon as definitive, rather than go into great detail. If ministers wish to consider certain subjects in greater depth, it might be appropriate to do so through the group of experts after this initial report has been submitted.

In each section of this chapter, standards are given where they exist. The Council and Ministries of Culture should consider the possibility of recommending existing standards, especially in the area of preservation where there are many, or of creating new ones where they are lacking. Any standard adopted should be considered as an ideal, a perfection to work towards, rather than as a directive which many Member States might for financial reasons find it difficult to fulfil.

2.1. BUILDINGS

Problems

Buildings and storage of archives are never far from the mind of the archivist, but current problems relate less to standards — of which there are several — than to the difficulties of persuading funding authorities, national or local, to provide appropriate accommodation.

Cooperation

There is little possibility of actual cooperation between Member States in this area, but Ministers for Culture may care to consider whether a statement of the general importance of archives should not include a reference to their proper accommodation, and to the acute difficulties occasionally faced by archivists from the lack of sufficient storage space.

Standards

There are several sets of criteria or recognized standards in this area:

- Michel Duchein's *Archive buildings and equipment*;
- British Standard BS 5454.

These vary slightly in detail, and also in emphasis, depending on whether they are aimed at funding authorities (BS 5454) or archivists and architects (Duchein). Otherwise there is little to choose between them, though Duchein is more widely known. The European Committee for Standardization and some other countries (Russia, Sweden, the Netherlands and Italy, for example) have produced standards.

Some are incomplete, some are only in draft, but all are at present under consideration by the ISO, which has formed a working group on document storage requirements. The standard it produces may take a year or two to complete.

2.2. STORAGE EQUIPMENT

Problems

While building standards generally have much to say on the question of equipment, the problems here are greater since there is more substandard equipment on the market — boxes and other containers which are not truly acid-free, shelves which bend too readily or are otherwise satisfactory, for example — and the market is an international one. In addition, the word 'archival', particularly in English, has been applied by manufacturers as a marketing term to products supposedly usable by archivists, for storage or conservation, but which fall far short of the appropriate standard. The word itself should be a guarantee of quality.

Cooperation

It is here rather than on buildings that some coordination would be both helpful and possible, perhaps by recommending both the ISO standard on paper (ISO 9706), and those parts of the standards listed in point 2.1 which relate to equipment rather than buildings themselves. Ministries' very reasonable concerns about acid-free paper, which might perhaps usefully extend to acid-free containers as well, should certainly include the use of appropriate storage within departments before material is transferred to an archive repository.

Standards

What has been said in point 2.1 for buildings applies equally here.

2.3. PERMANENT PAPER

Problems

The problems posed by the use of low-grade, often highly acid, paper are well known. They have been of particular concern to librarians for many years, and it is they who have invested most time and effort in trying to find effective methods of mass deacidification. Archivists must profit from their experience, but should avoid repeating their work. The major problem for archivists should be that of trying to ensure that good quality permanent paper is used for the creation of documents to be preserved. Acid paper, most fax paper, some of the papers used in photocopiers, and, unfortunately, recycled paper, are all for different reasons unsatisfactory for permanent preservation. The suggestion that archives on unsatisfactory paper should be transferred to microfilm so that the originals can be destroyed is a matter of professional ethics which is still under debate. It is also governed by the questions of cost, and of the unknown durability of microfilm.

Coordination

The recommendations set out on pages 14 and 15 of *The proceedings of the experts' meeting on conservation of acid paper material and the use of permanent paper*, National Preservation Office, The Hague, 1992 (published after the meeting organized in December 1991 by the European Commission in collaboration with the Dutch Presidency), should form the basis of any coordination. The group of experts on archives could insist particularly on Recommendation 5, that record-creating institutions should be encouraged to use permanent paper, and Recommendation 7, that publishers and the public in general should be made aware of the problem, and encouraged to do the same. At present, permanent paper is more expensive than ordinary paper, but this arises mainly from the fact that there is little demand for it. If demand increased, the cost would fall.

However, it is also pointed out at page 23 of the proceedings mentioned above that mass deacidification, a process from which some archive material could certainly benefit, is still a matter of much debate and in any case, because of its scientific complexity and cost, must essentially be a matter for international cooperation.[16]

Standards

The new international standard on paper quality (ISO 9706) should be adopted, and the recommendations of the abovementioned proceedings of the experts meeting should be set out as a plan of action in this matter.

2.4. NEW ARCHIVAL MATERIALS

Problems

The technical and professional treatment of moving images, photographs, machine-readable archives and sound recordings has been of concern to archivists for many years. Machine-readable archives will be discussed in Chapter 6, and photographs, though they present well-recognized conservation problems, are not a difficulty for the archivist in terms of their arrangement or exploitation.

But the problems associated particularly with audiovisual archives were discussed in detail by speakers at the 11 th International Congress on Archives, held at Paris

---

[16] In addition, several ways of dealing with the results of the use of acid paper are considered in *Papierzerfall*, the report of a Bund-Länder-Arbeitsgruppe, published in June 1992. Amongst other things, it considers conservation microfilming, and the costs of mass deacidification. In emphasizing the size of the problem, the report, like the Dutch one, encourages the development of international cooperation.

20

in 1988, and they have been set out again by Dietrich Schüller in 'Audiovisuelle Archivierung an der Schwelle des Digitalen Zeitalters' in *Das Audiovisuelle Archiv* Volume 27/28, Vienna, 1990. Technical difficulties have been discussed in a number of RAMP studies, and there is no lack of technical guidance on the management of archives in new forms, though there is still a lack of internationally accepted archival formats. But as far as audiovisual material is concerned, there remains the basic difficulty that most archives do not have either the specialist personnel or the specialist equipment needed for their effective exploitation. Archives have therefore tended — though with some very notable exceptions — to turn their back on them, and the preservation and exploitation of such materials have often become the responsibility of specialist repositories whose interests are not necessarily archival, and which can occasionally show scant regard for the needs of long-term preservation.

Cooperation

The root of this problem is of course financial, and it is possible that any EU funding available for archives should be directed towards this aspect of archive work. It might even be possible to consider the money so deployed as an investment, since there is no doubt that the exploitation of audiovisual archives can be turned into a source of revenue. But the growing interest in and availability of audiovisual material of all sorts mean that archives must involve themselves with it.

There is not at present any particular possibility of cooperation except at the level of discussions, whether bilateral or multilateral, to ensure that technical and professional information is widely available, and possibly with a view to creating internationally compatible formats. But it is a matter which must be set clearly before ministers as a subject of widespread concern.

Standards

There is an enormous technical literature on the subject of new archival materials, RAMP studies in particular. The papers produced for the 1988 Paris Congress of the ICA (which have been published) cover every aspect of the problems posed by audiovisual archives, but there do not appear to be any formal standards.

2.5. MICROFILM AND MICROFICHE

Problems

Some archival material, notably legal records, is automatically put on to microfilm or microfiche as part of the process of its creation, and exists only in that form. In these instances the problems are the same as those relating to archives preserved electronically. It is the message which is important rather than the medium, and it is therefore essential to ensure that the content of the material remains uncorrupted and intact as it is passed from one medium to another.

Where microfilm is created, or on occasion computer images are made, to serve as a substitute for the original, either for security reasons or for purposes of consultation, it is simply a matter of protecting fragile materials from excessive use and consequently from damage, and this is obviously something for local decision. But microfilm or microfiche can only replace original documents in exceptional and in some cases very precise circumstances, and the group would resist the suggestion occasionally made that archives should be transferred wholesale to microform so that they can be more easily stored.

Coordination

Some archives require microfilm of material preserved in other repositories which complement their own holdings. This is an area which principally concerns relations between the former colonial powers and their colonies; cooperation of this sort within the Community where it takes place is likely to be a simple bilateral arrangement.

Standards

Since the process of microfilm is in itself damaging to archive material, the objective must be to carry it out only once, and therefore to do it to the highest standard. ISO 4332 lays down the quality of reproduction which should be aimed for.

2.6. DISASTER PLANS

Problems

Nothing can make archive buildings completely secure against disaster. It is therefore important that each archive building should have a clearly established and well-understood procedure for dealing with any disaster which may occur.

Coordination

Disaster planning can only be carried out on a building-by-building basis, and is therefore not of itself open to harmonization, but when a disaster does occur, it should be assumed that the victim should be able to call, through the Commission, on the advice and expertise of any of the Member States. The international collaboration after the Florence floods in 1966 may serve as an example.

Standards

While no complete standard is possible in this area, there is no doubt that the type of equipment required to cope with disasters, and the immediate first-aid action that all staff should be able to undertake, can be set out. A practical and general guide is *Disaster planning, preparedness and recovery, for libraries and archives*, a RAMP study with guidelines, Paris, 1988.

22

2.7. THEFT

Problems

Though fine manuscripts have always been subject to theft, it is only in recent times that archive material has acquired a commercial value (autographs, postal history, etc.), and has thus offered a temptation to the thief. The special problems of private archives are dealt with elsewhere (see Chapter 8), but theft from public repositories is becoming increasingly serious. The literature on the subject emphasizes the need for vigilance in public areas, but some experience suggests that staff present as much of a problem as do the public.

Cooperation

As with disasters, there is not much room for cooperation, since the risks vary from country to country, and from archive building to building. However, it is essential:

(i) that experience should be shared, probably through publication in the professional literature;

(ii) that a description of material lost should be circulated at once in the way that stolen art objects are frequently described in art trade literature; and

(iii) that repositories should overcome their natural reluctance to do so, and publicize thefts widely as soon as they become apparent.

Standards

There appear to be no standards in this area, and, for example, the advantages of human over electronic surveillance or vice versa are still in debate. The matter is extensively covered by J.E. Simonet in two articles ('La protection contre le vol', and 'La securité contre le vol') in *Janus*, 1992, 1, pp. 62-68 and 101-105, and by William J. Stewart in 'Creating a secure archive', a paper presented at the meeting of the ICA/CBQ at Vienna in 1990.

2.8. RECOMMENDATIONS

2.8.1. That responsible authorities should take every opportunity of insisting on the importance of proper standards for buildings and archive storage.

2.8.2. That, until the forthcoming ISO standard has been promulgated, British Standard 5454 and Duchein's *Archive buildings and equipment* should be accepted as the ideal standard for archive buildings.

2.8.3. That equipment sold on the international market (paper, containers, shelving, etc.) should conform to ISO standard 9706 in the case of paper, and to the forthcoming ISO standard on archival storage for other materials.

2.8.4. That the word 'archival' should become a word which implies a particular standard of manufacture or performance.

2.8.5. That government departments which retain files during closure periods should be encouraged to keep them in archivally acceptable conditions.

2.8.6. That documentary material scheduled for permanent preservation should be on permanent paper.

2.8.7. That *The proceedings of the experts' meeting on conservation of acid paper material and the use of permanent paper* (The Hague, 1992) should be adopted by ministers and serve as a plan of action in this area.

2.8.8. That the international efforts currently being made to find an effective method of mass deacidification should be studied, and that the most satisfactory one should be adopted when it emerges, taking into account the work of the Member States in this area.

2.8.9. Archives should be encouraged to play an active role in the preservation and exploitation of audiovisual materials.

2.8.10. The Community should recognize the cost in terms of staff and equipment of the proper archival treatment of this material, and consider helping to fund it.

2.8.11. That the use of microform in place of originals for security or consultation purposes is a matter for local decision, but these microforms should be used as a substitute and only in exceptional cases as a replacement for originals.

2.8.12. That filming should be carried out only once, and to the highest standards (ISO 4332).

2.8.13. That there should exist a clearly stated and well-understood disaster plan for all archive buildings.

2.8.14. That, in the event of serious damage, conservation or other assistance should be available internationally.

2.8.15. That information about thefts, both what is stolen and how, should be published as fully and as soon as possible, and in particular other national archive services and appropriate authorities should be informed.

CHAPTER 3

THE PRACTICAL CONDITIONS OF ACCESS TO ARCHIVES

Archives are at the present time subject to profound changes in function. They are no longer simply preservation sites but are called upon to offer an extensive range of services to their users, the typology of which has broadened to encompass all interested citizens. Archives have, at present, a cultural and informative function, the scale of which has led them to turn increasingly to new information techniques and new technological resources.

The National Archives therefore have to devote themselves to responding even more comprehensively to the needs of all archives users, by offering the latter — within the limits of their financial means and without forgetting the requirements linked with the preservation and integrity of irreplaceable documents — the optimum practical conditions for consultation.

The national legislation of each Member State and the regulations in force in repositories should encourage access and free movement by the users, avoiding as far as possible access formalities which are either too complicated, which discriminate against foreigners or which are too expensive.

Finally, pragmatic research, taking experience and the principle of subsidiarity into account, could be carried out within the Community, with a view to codifying the rules of access and to implementing official arrangements concerning the following priorities: archival description standards, exchanging archival copies, making national computerized systems and models compatible.

In so far as practical conditions of access are concerned, the regulations and traditions in existence in the Member States are marked by a significant diversity, according to the sociocultural heritage of each country and its financial means in this sphere. Within the context of increased opening of the archives, however, it is important to respond even more effectively to the needs of all archive users. The organization of access and services must offer suitable surroundings for consultation and avoid discriminatory treatment, particularly between national and non-national users, at no time losing sight of the requirements linked with the preservation and integrity of irreplaceable documents.

3.1. ACCESS FORMALITIES AND PRACTICAL METHODS OF SUPPLYING DOCUMENTS, ETC.

All the Member States have regulations for practical methods of supplying documents and in particular for discipline in reading rooms. These regulations are sometimes in force in all the repositories which are responsible to the National Archives (Belgium, Italy, the Netherlands), but more often relate to a single archive repository (Germany, Spain, France, Greece, Ireland, Portugal, the United Kingdom).

• Concerning access formalities, apart from certain indispensable security measures (proof of readers' identity is required virtually everywhere), complicated authorization procedures, in theory, no longer apply. However, access to the archives of the Ministries of Foreign Affairs and/or Defence often remains subject to a specific regulation requiring authorization from the embassy and/or a letter of introduction from directors of research (Germany, Portugal, France, Greece, Spain, for example).

With concern for openness and fairness, the experts unanimously reject the application of a principle of reciprocity with regard to access to National Archives.

On the other hand they would like to encourage approximation of the authorization procedures for consultation, with the idea that a single authorization may eventually be valid for all the National Archives of the Member States and of the EC institutions.

Most of the experts recommend that the clause relating to 'the most-favoured nation' be applicable, with regard to consultation, to users living in the Member States.

The delegates, by a large majority, firmly oppose payment for access, which could be considered to be a contravention of the free inspection allowed by law. The French and Portuguese delegates would, nevertheless, consent to users being asked to make a modest contribution, designed to cover, at cost price, the use of equipment or specialist services (examination of databases, detailed research, for example). In the United Kingdom the question of charging for services, including access to the collections, is being discussed with a view to determining when it is reasonable to expect the user of a service to pay for it and when it is reasonable to expect the taxpayer to do so.

• The conditions of consultation are not always and everywhere in tune with users' expectations.

The disadvantages resulting from such deficiencies increase in proportion with the distance between the archives and the reader's home. Foreigners, who often represent up to 25% of the total presence in the consultation rooms, find themselves particularly penalized.

A general extension of working sessions is noted and the National Archives are trying more often to keep the reading rooms open during holiday periods. Ideally, the reading rooms should be accessible for at least 40 hours a week, spread over six days a week (whereas at the present time the national repositories are open between 30 and 70 hours a week, depending on the Member State and the repository). It should be possible to consult users regarding the hours which would best suit them, in accordance with local conditions.

- The group believes that it is possible for the National Archives, as a result of their workforce and technical possibilities, to reduce the time taken to supply a document and to take account of readers' desires regarding the number of files supplied to the users.

Minimum arrangements should only be recommended in accordance with whether the archives under consideration are national or local. The constraints on certain national repositories, moving several tonnes of archives a day, cannot be compared with those on local archive services.

As a general principle, nearly all archive repositories would prefer that nothing penalizes the number of articles requested for consultation by the reader in one day, as long as this is compatible with service potential. With the aim of alleviating the constraints on the latter, restraining readers' excessive requests and preventing them disordering the files, most Member States have anticipated a limit to the number of items supplied per consultation request. This number, which the group suggests as a standard minimum, is usually three.

Another way of reducing the time taken to supply documents would be to request these in advance by letter. In France, documents are reserved at the National Archives in Paris through the Minitel service.

3.2. REPROGRAPHIC SERVICES

Reprographic services are amongst the most widespread methods of disseminating archives. These services should be supplied by the National Archives in accordance with the following criteria at least:

(i) a range of reprographic processes, as full as possible, should be available to users of the National Archives: photocopying (daily service if possible) copies or prints of microforms (in self-service form), microfilming and photography;

(ii) preservation needs are recognized to be the priority in relation to those of reproduction.

The National Archives should expand the exchanges of copies of archives (microfilms, microfiche) relating to the history of a country other than that of the place of preservation.

Microfilm reproduction systems should be available to the public, at least in the large repositories.

3.3. ASSISTANCE TO THE USERS

3.3.1. Guides and research tools (published or unpublished)

Access to the archives depends essentially upon the production and distribution of guides to the repositories, inventories, indexes, examination systems, etc.

- These research tools are not generally standardized. In Western Europe it is often through the professional associations and/or communal archival training that the harmonization of methods of classification and development of research tools (as suggested in the chapter on the exchange of information) takes place. International standards of archival description which are at present in the process of development could be adopted and recognized by the Member States.

- The low level of distribution of research tools, also the fact that a number of them are not kept up to date, are probably two of the most significant obstacles to access to the archives.

In several of the Member States, programmes of indexation of 'Guides to the repositories and to the spheres of jurisdiction and operation of the organizations which produced the preserved collections' have been produced or are in the process of development. In France, indexation of the French public archives research tools is standardized (tables of geographic division and of subject-matter, compatible thesaurus). Such programmes should be sustained and coordinated in such a way that their international distribution is facilitated. Each Member State should publish and distribute a guide to its collections in various forms (printed, on-line, floppy disk, hard disk and microfiche).

- In several Member States access to documents is hindered by the absence of an inventory or even a summary of the material placed in the archives, which is a result of the fact that the National Archives are clogged by masses of unclassified public archives.

The fact that no research tool exists for a collection should not be used as an excuse to prevent access. In some Member States it is preferred that researchers are given summarized research tools rather than waiting for a complete inventory to be published before making the material available. This policy should be recommended to all Member States.

- Is it necessary to translate the guides and research tools? Research tools published by the National Archives are only translated in exceptional circumstances. In the Netherlands, some inventories of collections which are of significant interest to foreign researchers are published in French and English or provided with a summary in a language other than Dutch. In Belgium, inventories are published in French or Dutch and in Luxembourg in French or German. Denmark allows for the possibility of summary translations when the inventories relate to a foreign State. The Scottish Record Office has published a repository guide in French.

The obstacle to translation is essentially financial, but some experts question the actual use of translations of research tools in view of the fact that the user is obliged to read the documents in the language of the country visited. However, most of the experts consider that it would be preferable to encourage the exchange of inventories (if possible in several languages) of international interest.

- Several Member States say that they are ready to exchange the inventories which they publish but nothing is really organized on a European scale. Denmark already exchanges its research tools with those of several Member States. The Netherlands indicates the possibility of lending, even abroad, the published inventories. France only provides for exchanges between French archive services; it no longer distributes the research tools concerning regional and local archives to foreign countries but continues to distribute research tools relating to the national archives to the National Archives of Member States. There is a tendency noted everywhere — which should be encouraged — to exchanges between border regions. This exchange is likely to be facilitated on a European scale.

A culturally strong community could eventually envisage the creation of a telematic network allowing remote access or automatic exchange of inventories, by agreeing the use of standards of description and conditions of data access and by seeking greater compatibility of national computer systems and models. In Spain, a database is in the process of development for the exchange of archival information.

- The idea — put into practice by the archives of the French Ministry of Foreign Affairs — of producing bilingual user guides (in the national language and English, for example) for the use of newly registered readers, allowing them to find their bearings and familiarize themselves with the organization of an archives service, should be considered everywhere.

Specialized guides have appeared over several decades, which summarize all the documents of the same kind or relating to a given subject which are placed in the repositories of one country. The Community could organize a collection of similar guides. In particular such a step could lead to the publication of an 'Archival guide to the history of Europe' (as exists for the history of several Member States). The 'Guide to diplomatic sources of European cooperation', edited by the archives of the Italian Ministry of Foreign Affairs, constitutes a model in this respect.

3.3.2. Regulations and discipline in the reading rooms

This relates to practical arrangements against the theft of documents and preventive measures for the preservation of the documents supplied, such as respect for certain rules of handling. These measures arise from the idea that the first duty of the National Archives is to preserve, and preferably preserve in a good state. It is also with this aim in mind that many countries prohibit the supply of original documents when these are too old, too fragile or likely to be used too frequently (old civil status registers, parish registers, etc.).

However, the fragility or deterioration of a document is not a criterion for refusing access indefinitely. If access must be refused temporarily until reproduction on a substitute medium, the user should be notified of the date when the substitute form of the document will be available.

3.3.3. Information service

The National Archives are having to receive ever-increasing numbers of the general public and familiarize them with access procedures, including research tools.

The National Archives must be in a position to respond to the requirements and needs of the readers and researchers. For this reason:

- responses to written requests must be sent in reasonable time, varying more in accordance with the specific nature of the research to be carried out than with the responsibilities and obligations of the department called upon;
- requests for information from users in the reading room (whether these relate to the facilities of the institution, the research tools or the archives themselves) must be satisfied there and then by trained personnel (scientifically organized);
- all reading room personnel should receive training which is orientated towards receiving readers.

3.4. RECOMMENDATIONS

3.4.1. That Community users of the National Archives should be treated on an equal footing.

3.4.2. That reading rooms at the National Archives should be accessible for at least 40 hours per week.

3.4.3. That the National Archives should, ideally, not limit the number of items requested for consultation by the readers. A limit of three items per consultation request is nevertheless envisaged.

3.4.4. That a full range of reprographic processes should be available and a system of exchange through reproduction should be encouraged.

3.4.5. That each Member State should publish and distribute a bilingual user guide.

3.4.6. That each archive repository should have available a published repository guide.

3.4.7. That the absence of a full inventory should not prevent researchers from having access to an archival collection.

3.4.8. That the exchange of inventories of collections of international interest should be encouraged.

3.4.9. That the Community should encourage the creation of an archival telematic network.

3.4.10. That minimum provisions for the services to be given to readers and researchers should be recommended to the National Archives.

3.4.11. That all reading room personnel should receive training orientated towards receiving readers.

3.5. MONITORING PROPOSALS

The implementation of the above recommendations would necessarily involve additional expense, which should be taken into account at the time of budget allocations for both regional and national archives.

- The group expresses the hope that these recommendations will serve as a basis for assessing the allocation of more sizeable budgets to allow their implementation.
- The group considers that it would be useful to carry out studies with a view to formulating practical recommendations with regard to access on the level of the Member States. Those spheres which would lend themselves easily to harmonization would be chosen in accordance with four criteria: urgency, the existence of an agreement in principle already ratified by archival practice, correlation with the concerns previously expressed by the ICA, respect for the principle of subsidiarity.

With regard to practical access, the following priority areas could be opted for: archival description standards, exchanges of copies of archives, making national computer systems and models compatible.

CHAPTER 4

NATIONAL LEGISLATION AND ACCESS TO ARCHIVES

The legislation of the various Member States places certain limits on free access to administrative documents, by imposing either a general period of delay or specific periods for various categories of archives.

In spite of the diversity of archival legislation within the various Member States, they have adopted a general period of delay before access to the archives of 30 years, even less. This is the case in particular in the Netherlands, which has adopted a narrower period of 20 years. The period of 30 years should thus be considered to be the maximum, namely a ceiling rather than a threshold.

With regard to access periods for the archives, it is not possible to ignore specific legislation not strictly concerned with archives. Thus the legislation of several Member States explicitly provides that the citizen has free access to administrative documents from the time of their creation. However, on the other hand, some categories of archives elude general legislation regarding access, either because they form the object of special stipulations regarding the protection of privacy or State security or because they are covered by legislative provisions which are separate from those of archival legislation.

Exceptional dispensations regarding access are granted in several Member States, but they are not always governed by specific legal provisions. In the same way, the process of classification and declassification of certain confidential documents could clearly be established through national legislation.

With regard to exceptions to access, each Member State must at least endeavour to draw up a list, as detailed as possible, summarizing the types of document which will only be accessible after the general period prescribed by the law. This will avoid, in so far as possible, any arbitrariness which may prejudice the rights of the citizen and the ease of research. In addition to this work on the openness of each Member State, useful work of alignment could be undertaken within the Community by collecting together the lists of exceptions and possibly adapting them in common within an archival agreement, which would also take into account the problem of copyright, as it exists in the sphere of archives. Such action would serve to clarify the problem of access periods and to reconcile jointly the right to information and the necessity of protecting certain information for periods as long as 30 years.

4.1. THE PROBLEM OF ACCESS TO ARCHIVES

All the Member States possess laws and regulations (general or specific) which lay down the conditions of public access to archives (see Annex 1).

The relevance of applying a firm legal basis to the access to archives rests notably on the following considerations:

(a) a legal basis is necessary in order to ensure the preservation of documents deemed to be archives, originating from diverse responsible authorities, thus preventing their possible destruction;

(b) the right of the citizen to consult archives of administrative origin should be legally guaranteed;

(c) the development of the law relating to the protection of data, during the course of recent decades, has required that the functions of public archives be legally described as part of the public administration. The restrictions of the law relating to the protection of data must be offset by special regulations in order to be able to take due account of the reasons and rights of the citizen to use archives, without prejudicing the interests, which merit protection, of the person concerned;

(d) Legal provisions relating to the confidentiality of documents are not only a barrier to their consultation in the archives, but are an obstacle to consultation from the moment of their transmission. Legal provisions relating to archives should therefore establish an appropriate balance between the right of access and the right to privacy and to confidentiality for other reasons.

But the definition itself of the word 'archives' varies from one Member State to another, which makes these comparisons difficult.

In Spain, France and Greece all documents produced or received by a department, an institution or any organization whatsoever, are equally defined as archives. In these Member States, access to the archives relates not only to documents which are effectively preserved in the archives, but also those which are preserved by the archive-producing department. Elsewhere, access to archives only concerns those documents actually preserved in the archive repositories.

4.2. THE BASIC PRINCIPLES OF ACCESS TO ARCHIVES

In all the Community Member States, the right of the public to have access to the information contained in archival documents is recognized by law.

In four of the 12 Member States (Spain, Italy, Luxembourg, the Netherlands), all the documents preserved in the National Archives can, in principle, be consulted freely, with exceptions which will be studied later (see point 4.4). This has the logical implication that only documents which are able to be inspected are placed in the National Archives.

In seven other Member States (Germany, Denmark, France, Greece, Ireland, Portugal, the United Kingdom), documents can be consulted at the end of a period of 30 years from their creation, with exceptions which will be studied later. This period of 30 years results from experience and from the desire to establish a suitable balance between the right of access to the archives on the one hand, and the rights designed to protect human personality, the interests of State security and efficient administration, on the other hand (even though these two latter arguments have frequently lost much of their value).

It is not a rigid period, however, since it can be shortened or lengthened. [17]

In Belgium, no recent general legislation seems to exist stipulating the conditions of access to archives, but internal regulations and specific legislation for certain categories of documents do exist.

4.3. FREEDOM OF ACCESS TO ADMINISTRATIVE DOCUMENTS

Five Member States of the Community have adopted, in the course of the last 15 years, laws of the Freedom of Information Act type (Denmark, 1985; Greece, 1986; France, 1979; Italy, 1990; the Netherlands, 1978 and 1991). The Spanish constitution guarantees, in Article 105B, the right of access to administrative documents, but no implementing decree has even been adopted.

These laws do not make reference to archives already placed in the National Archives. On the other hand, the methods of access which they define for administrative documents are very different from one Member State to another, as well as the definition of documents which may be consulted.

4.4. RESTRICTIONS ON THE RIGHT OF ACCESS

All national European legislation and regulations contain provisions for restricting access to certain categories of documents, in order to protect certain rights and legitimate interests of persons, authorities, enterprises and the State.

The definition of these categories varies considerably from one Member State to another, which makes comparison of them difficult. They can, however, be grouped under three principal headings.

---

[17] The legislation of the various German *Länder* confirms this tendency to standardize access periods around a key period of 30 years. However, the 'Thüringische Archivgesetz' removes this 30-year protection period for GDR documents which do not concern persons (Article 17, paragraph 2). With regard to Schleswig-Holstein, the protection period of 10 years constitutes the normal period.
By virtue of the BArchG (Bundesarchivgesetz) and the laws relating to archives of the *Länder*, the 30-year period can be prolonged by 30 years at maximum if this is in the public interest. This possibility has never — or very rarely — been used up to now with regard to Federal and *Länder* archives.

4.4.1. The protection of personal privacy

All the Member States protect personal privacy against the indiscretions which could result from premature availability of administrative documents concerning people, either under general laws relating to the protection of privacy, or under specific laws relating to archives or administrative documents. Unfortunately, the idea of 'privacy' has never been precisely defined, so that restrictions on the availability of documents vary markedly from one Member State to another. [18]

BELGIUM

Documents originating from the courts and from solicitors are made available 100 years after their creation.

DENMARK

Documents containing information of a confidential nature relating to persons can be made available 80 years after the date of the documents.

GERMANY

- Documents 'relating to physical persons': can be made available 30 years after the death of those concerned, or (if the date of death is not known) 110 years after birth. [19]
- Documents 'of which there are reasons to suppose that they may be damaging to the legitimate interests of third parties': period not specified.
- Documents which fall within the scope of Federal legal provisions relating to confidentiality (particularly social and taxation laws): the archives are closed for 80 years.

GREECE

Documents relating to the private lives of persons can be made available after advice from the National Archives.

SPAIN

- Documents 'containing personal information of a police, legal or medical nature or other information which could affect the safety of persons, their honour, the privacy of their private and family lives or their personal image': can be made available 25 years after the death of those concerned, or (if the date of death is not known) 50 years after the date of the documents.
- Solicitors' documents: 100 years after the date of the documents.

---

[18] In so far as legislation on databases which contain personal information is concerned, we refer to Chapter 5, which relates to computer archives (machine-readable data).

[19] The majority of the Länder laws concerning archives stipulate, without prejudice to the protection period of 30 years which is the norm, shorter periods, namely 10 years after death or 90 years after birth.

FRANCE

- Documents of civil status, solicitors' documents, judicial documents: 100 years after the date of the documents.
- Individual personal files: 120 years after the birth of those concerned.
- Named medical documents: 150 years after the birth of those concerned.
- Police documents containing information relating to the private lives of persons: 60 years after the date of the documents.
- Tax documents containing information on the wealth or private lives of persons: 60 years after the date of the documents.

IRELAND

Documents 'which if made available to the public would be damaging or dangerous for living persons', or which contain information on the private lives of persons, or which are likely to provoke defamation proceedings, or which contain information obtained by the authority under the promise of confidentiality: availability period laid down by the certifying officer of the producing department with the approval of the consenting officer in the Department of the Taoiseach; the Taoiseach may authorize exceptions for the consultation of these documents.

ITALY

- Documents relating to the 'purely private lives of persons': 70 years after the date of the documents.
- Documents of criminal proceedings: 70 years after the date of the proceedings.

LUXEMBOURG

Documents of a nature to undermine the honour of individuals or of families: availability period laid down by the Director of the State Archives.

NETHERLANDS

- Documents to which free access would constitute prejudice to the privacy of persons: their availability is restricted by specific conditions, laid down by the archive-producing department on the advice of the archivist.
- Legal or taxation documents, documents of civil status (marriage certificates): the period after which they can be placed in the repositories of the National Archives is 75 years after the date of the document (whereas documents are usually placed at the end of 20 years).[20]
- Documents of civil status (birth certificates): the period for placing of these archives in the repositories of the National Archives is 100 years.

---

[20] This period, currently 50 years, will be lowered to 20 years at the beginning of 1995.

PORTUGAL

Documents containing judicial, police or clinical records of individuals are not to be communicated. The same treatment applies to those containing confidential personal data on individuals, or information that could in any way affect the safety, honour or the intimacy of their private and family life as well as their image, unless personal data may be removed from the document containing it, without any danger of the individual being recognized; unless the individuals whose rights are to be protected have given their consent; or, unless 50 years have passed since the date of death of the person to whom they refer, or if this is unknown 75 years after the date of the documents.

UNITED KINGDOM

Documents containing 'information obtained under the promise of confidentiality', documents containing 'information concerning persons, the divulgence of which would be prejudicial or dangerous to living persons or their immediate descendants': availability period laid down by the Lord Chancellor upon a proposal from the Keeper of Public Records in England, and in Scotland by the archive-producing department, after consultation with the Keeper of the Records of Scotland (in practice, from 50 to 100 years, according to the documents).

The national laws on the protection of privacy present significant divergences, which have consequences for archival operations. The Commission has proposed a draft directive of which the amended version is at the discussion stage by a Council working party. This draft sums up the general principles of protection of privacy already mentioned in the Council of Europe Convention No 108, as well as in several national laws. One of these principles, that personal data 'should only be preserved in a form allowing identification of the persons concerned for a duration which does not exceed that necessary for carrying out the objectives sought', clashes with archival rules if it is interpreted too strictly. It is important that archival preservation is included in the exceptions to this principle allowed in the draft, which provide that 'appropriate guarantees should be provided by the Member States for data of a personal nature which is preserved for reasons of history, statistics or science'. Except perhaps in very exceptional and well-specified cases, it is necessary to prevent general national laws on the protection of privacy from prohibiting the preservation of data of a personal nature for archival ends. More extensive consultation of archivists would be necessary in this connection.

4.4.2. The protection of the interests of the State and public security

The restrictions on access designed to protect the interests of the State and public security are in general set forth in a fairly vague way. However, certain Member States (particularly France) give these a more precise and detailed definition.

BELGIUM

Documents 'concerning State security and national defence, the fundamental financial and economic interests of the State and other bodies under public law, the maintenance of public order and security, investigations and proceedings relating to punishable actions': periods not specified.

DENMARK

Documents 'concerning State security, the defence of the Kingdom, the protection of the political and economic interests of the State and public enterprises': periods to be laid down by the Director of the National Archives in agreement with the archive-producing department.

GERMANY (Bundesarchiv)

Documents of which divulgence 'would constitute a threat to the interests of the Federal Republic or one of its *Länder*': period not specified; these documents are normally classified 'secret' and can be made available after declassification.

GREECE

Documents 'which if made available to the public could damage the national interest': period laid down by the Director of the National Archives after advice from the Archives Advisory Council.

SPAIN

There are no specified periods for documents classified in accordance with the Law of Official Secrets (Ley de Secretos Oficiales) or for documents of which 'the dissemination of its contents could involve risks for the security and defence of the State or with regard to investigating crime', by virtue of Article 57.I.a. of the Law of the Spanish Historical Heritage (Ley de Patrimonio Historico Español). However, it is possible to ask for an administrative authorization for access to documents which are not freely available. This authorization concerning secret and restricted documents can be obtained by the authority which has made this declaration, and in other cases, by the head of department responsible, by virtue of Article 57.I.b. of the abovementioned Ley de Patrimonio Historico Español.

FRANCE

- Archives of the President of the Republic and the Prime Minister: 60 years after the date of the documents.
- Archives of the Minister for the Interior and the Police regarding State security or national defence: 60 years after the date of the documents.
- Documents relating to financial, monetary and commercial negotiations with foreign countries: 60 years after the date of the documents.
- Military or diplomatic documents classified 'defence secret' or 'highly secret': 60 years after the date of the documents (also the various military and diplomatic

documents listed in Article 6 of Decree No 79-1035 of 3 December 1979 and Article 8 of Decree No 80-975 of 1 December 1980).

IRELAND

Documents whose divulgence 'would be against the public interest': periods laid down by the certifying officer of the producing department with the approval of the consenting officer in the Department of the Taoiseach; the Taoiseach may authorize exceptions for the consultation of these documents.

ITALY

Documents 'of a reserved nature relating to the foreign or home policy of the State': 50 years after the date of the documents.

LUXEMBOURG

Documents whose availability 'appears to be of a nature to present disadvantages from an administrative point of view': availability period laid down by the Director of the State Archives.

NETHERLANDS

Documents whose divulgence would constitute a threat to State security or to the relationships of the Netherlands with other States or with international organizations, and documents containing industrial information which have been submitted to the government under the seal of secrecy: availability restricted by specific conditions, laid down by the archive-producing department upon advice from the archivist.

PORTUGAL

Documents 'relating to State security and constitutional defence': availability laid down by the government department from which the documents emanated.

UNITED KINGDOM

Documents whose divulgence 'would be contrary to public interest for reasons of security or other reasons, including taxation matters': availability period laid down by the Lord Chancellor upon a proposal from the Keeper of Public Records in England, and in Scotland by the archive-producing department, after consultation with the Keeper of the Records of Scotland (in practice, from 50 to 100 years, according to the documents).

4.4.3. The protection of economic interests of individuals and enterprises

The archive laws of the Member States of the Community are in general rather imprecise concerning availability periods for documents relating to the commercial, industrial and financial interests of enterprises and individuals. The laws which lay down these periods (or which set out the restrictions upon access) are specific laws: laws on industrial ownership, on invention patents, on economic espionage, etc. The periods, when they are specified by law, are in general from 30 to 60 years (80 years in Germany).

4.4.4. The protection of copyright

Copyright is protected in all the Member States of the Community. Although archivists are not alone in being concerned with protection of copyright, it is necessary to define the types of documents which are or are not subject to copyright. The document produced outside a public service which, if it were printed, would be subject to protection is, of course, to be protected. The copying of documents of this kind is subject to authorization by the author. Specific cases (for example: the publication of letters, exhibition of documents) are of course to be handled by analogy with similar cases in the private and/or commercial sector.

A joint group, composed of experts on copyright and archivists, should analyse in detail the regulations in force in the various Member States of the Community and reconcile, notably with regard to copyright as applied to archives, the interests of both the authors and the researchers, the latter having a right to the information. This joint group could then develop a new and uniform arrangement.

4.4.5. Specific legislation

It should not be forgotten that many restrictions upon access to documents do not emanate from the archive laws, but from specific laws which are not always well known by archivists and which are not always easily aligned with the archive laws:

laws on national defence, the protection of the State, etc.,

laws on public order, the investigation of crimes and offences, etc.,

laws on the administration of justice,

laws on civil status and personal status,

laws on medicine, hospitals, social security, etc.,

laws on taxation, customs, etc.,

laws on statistical secrecy,

laws on industrial and commercial secrecy, copyright, etc.,

laws on the protection of individual data, such as the protection of personal data,

international treaties.

A detailed study of these laws is outside the context of this chapter, but it is certain that genuine harmonization of European legislation concerning access to archives would involve such a study, exceeding the context of archive legislation as such.

4.5. EXCEPTIONAL AUTHORIZATION PROCEDURES RELATING TO ACCESS TO DOCUMENTS WHICH ARE NOT FREELY AVAILABLE

In principle, all national legislation should clearly define the procedures for exceptional authorization for access to documents which are not freely available. This is unfortunately not the case everywhere.

BELGIUM

There is no specific legal provision. The Ministry of Scientific Policy as successor of the Ministry of Public Education 'determines the procedures in accordance with which documents are made available to researchers'.

DENMARK

The Director of the National Archives can authorize access to documents before expiry of the periods laid down, in agreement with the archive-producing department, or, if it concerns computerized files, with the Computerized Files Committee (Registertilsyn). Divulgence of the information contained in documents made available in this way is strictly controlled.

GERMANY (Bundesarchiv)

- The 30-year availability period can be shortened by the Bundesarchiv with agreement from those concerned. Similar methods exist in the *Länder*.
- In the case of archival documents and items relating to persons, the periods may be shortened with agreement from the persons concerned. If this condition is not fulfilled the availability periods can nevertheless be shortened:
  - (a) if consultation of the archival documents and items is essential to scientific research or in order to prove the existence of the rights of a person or authority and if any prejudice to the interests deemed to be protected can be excluded;
  - (b) with regard to the personalities of modern history and public officials in the exercise of their duties, the protection period can be reduced as long as the interests of the persons concerned, which are deemed to be protected, are duly taken into consideration.

  As for the general period of 30 years, the right to decide upon a reduction in the period with regard to those archival documents and items concerning persons is a matter for the Federal archives. In this case, again, it requires agreement from the person concerned for documents produced since 1949.
- Documents which come under the legal provisions of the Federal government regarding secrecy can only be used 80 years after their creation.[21] Unlike the other protection periods, these documents are subject to absolute protection. In most of the legislation by the *Länder* regarding archives, the protection period

---

21 See Annex 4: Paragraph 203 of the German Penal Code on the violation of private secrets.

relating to the archives formed in accordance with the legislation of the *Land* and subject to the secrecy provision is only 60 years, this period being able to be reduced.

GREECE

There is no specific legal provision.

SPAIN

There is no specific legal provision. In practice, authorizations are granted by the head of the archive-producing department. If documents of a personal nature are involved, the authorization of the person concerned is compulsorily required.

FRANCE

The Director of the National Archives grants 'dispensation' authorizations (the release of documents which are not freely available) after agreement from the archive-producing department. The copying and divulgence of documents made available in this way are strictly controlled. In some rare categories 'general dispensations' exist which are issued in agreement with the departments concerned.

IRELAND

'A member of the government can authorize access to documents emanating from its departments before the expiry of the 30-year period.'

ITALY

The Ministry of the Interior can authorize, for research purposes (per motivi di studio), the release of documents which are not freely available.

LUXEMBOURG

There is no specific legal provision.

NETHERLANDS

The Ministry of Culture can authorize the consultation of documents which are not freely available if it is acknowledged that the interests of research are greater than those of the restrictions upon access.

PORTUGAL

Exceptional authorizations are issued by those institutions or services from which the documents emanated.

UNITED KINGDOM

'Access to documents which are not freely available is at the discretion of the Ministries from which the documents emanated.'

4.6. RESTRICTIONS ON ACCESS FOR THE PHYSICAL PROTECTION OF DOCUMENTS

Only four Member States (Germany, Greece, the Netherlands and Portugal) possess legal or statutory provisions allowing refusal of release of documents which are at risk as a result of their fragility or poor state of preservation. In this case it is generally — but not always — specified that if the original document cannot be made available a photograph or a photocopy must be made available to the public.

However, in spite of the silence of most archive laws on this point, it seems that refusal to hand over documents in poor condition is quite generally practised.

4.7. INSPECTION OF DOCUMENTS FROM PRIVATE ARCHIVES

No law amongst the 12 Member States governs public access to private archives, this access being left to the discretion of the owners.

Italian legislation provides, however, that researchers must have access to private archives which are classified as being of 'particular historical interest' (di notevole interesse storico). Nevertheless, this legal provision is difficult to apply in practice if the owners refuse.

When private archives enter public archive repositories, by donation or legacy, the donors or legatees can place conditions upon the inspection of these archives. On the other hand, when it is a question of purchases, the documents thus acquired by the National Archives are normally made available under the same conditions as the documents of public archives.

4.8. CONCLUSIONS AND PROPOSALS

The preceding account shows, on the one hand, the profound similarity of the legal and ethical principles which govern the availability of archives in the 12 Member States of the Community and, on the other hand, the great diversity of formulas adopted by the laws and regulations of these 12 Member States regarding the concrete expression of these principles.

It seems illusory (and moreover in the main useless) to seek complete unification of these laws and regulations, many of which are connected with ideas and traditions which are specific to each national culture. However, it could be wished that where analogous documents of all countries are concerned, the rules of access be harmonized, with duly justified exceptions. This harmonization could relate in particular to:

- documents of civil status (100 years after the date of the document, in order to protect personal privacy, taking account of the increased longevity of the European population);

- individual personal files (100 years after birth, for the same reasons as above).

The regulations in force regarding copyright could also be harmonized in order to reconcile, through joint action, the protection of copyright with the rights of archive users.

For other documents (medical, legal, taxation documents, etc.) meetings of experts could succeed, by comparing the various legislation and regulations in detail, in formulating harmonization proposals, but it should not be concealed that such work would touch upon many spheres other than that of archives and could come up against solid legal, psychological and even constitutional obstacles.

On the other hand, a European definition of personal data, which is essential for clarifying the conditions of access to archives, would be eminently desirable and would fill an evident gap in present law. It would also be desirable for the national laws on privacy, which will be introduced following the Council Directive, to take sufficient account of archival interests.

The same applies to conditions of access to documents which are not freely available: clarification of the procedures on this point would ensure greater openness and avoid the reproach from researchers in various countries that they are arbitrary, at the same time preserving the principle of non-availability with regard to documents whose divulgence could injure the legitimate interests of persons, authorities, enterprises or States.

CHAPTER 5

THE MANAGEMENT AND STORAGE OF COMPUTERIZED ARCHIVES

Are we to witness a loss of memory in computerized societies?

Through lack of time and means and through failure of adequate preparation for the consequences of the revolution in information technology, the archive-producing departments pay too little attention to permanent preservation of their computerized archives.

In addition, the fear of seeing information technology seriously threaten privacy has led the governments of a number of Member States to legislate in this sphere. The law provides more and more often for systematic destruction of databases when divulgence of the personal data which they contain could affect citizens' privacy. In this debate archivists have rarely succeeded in making themselves heard.

Even when computerized archives are preserved, it is difficult to discern where they come from, as a result of the ease with which these sources can be contaminated by several successive or simultaneous producers; this could, if care is not taken, threaten one of the fundamental archival principles. Here again, archival views are heard with difficulty in the search for the establishment of standards in information technology.

Finally, the rapid development of information technology means that archivists have to keep up incessantly with the most recent progress at the same time as preserving the memory of obsolete programmes and machines.

Joint action on a European level would give more coherence to national experiments in this sphere of archives. Much wasted effort could be spared by seeking active collaboration between the Member States, based on the principle of subsidiarity. The objective is to achieve a general model for the management of computerized archives, which implies a certain level of harmonization, the setting of specific preservation standards, control of access, the choice of appropriate infrastructure and, if necessary, a defined regulation regarding consultation of the databases.

It is necessary beforehand to make a survey of the research in progress and then gather together the results which are already obtained. There are grounds for promoting a programme of concerted research on a Community level, avoiding wasting energy and means. This Community research programme should also be concerned with the physical control of computerized archives, an area in which results should be obtained very easily.

5.1. A NEW CONTEXT

The authorities preserve in memory data which is both a working tool and the result of their operations. They do not necessarily take into account the subsequent use of this data, for example in historical research. It is considered that a relatively small proportion of the documents produced or received by the authorities, generally between 3 and 5%, is usually preserved as being of cultural and historical interest.

During the course of recent years we have witnessed a distinct growth in the use of computer technology by the archive-producing authorities, which has strongly influenced their operations. Thus computer-retained data has been created, amended, exchanged and stored differently from that retained by traditional methods.

Certain signs demonstrate that the use of information technology is in the process of provoking a more and more distinct split between the use of data for carrying out administrative functions and the subsequent management of the computerized archives which result from this.[22] The rapid development of computer techniques evidently accentuates the problem. The organizations concerned, which already carry out access to current data with difficulty, somewhat neglect other interests such as the cultural and historical interest of computerized data. In the short term, the problem is the preservation of information which is no longer current on an administrative level but still necessary with regard to legal responsibilities. In the longer term the protection of a cultural and historical source is at stake. In the worst hypothesis, this situation could lead to what might be termed a loss of memory by the archive-producing institutions. Could the last quarter of the 20th century be the worst documented period in history?

Even when passed on to the National Archives, computerized data encounter a new problem, that of legibility and interpretation of the material. The main difference from paper preservation of information is that digital storage of data does not allow the latter to be read or interpreted without the aid of software or hardware.

Finally, here again there is a particularly acute problem regarding the protection of personal data, as mentioned in Chapter 4. There is a real fear of witnessing information technology becoming an easy way of divulging personal data, thus representing a threat to privacy. This fear has led to the recommendation in some cases of destruction of the databases in question, although they would merit preservation from an archival point of view given the required precautions. More than in the past, archivists should be involved in the reflection necessary in this respect.

---

[22] See, amongst others, *Management of electronic records — issues and guidelines*, New York, 1990 (report of the Advisory Committee on the coordination of United Nations information systems (ACCIS)); and the work of Margaret Hedstrom, 'Understanding electronic incunabula: a framework for the research on electronic records' (in *The American Archivist*, Volume 54, 1991, pp. 336-337).

5.2. MARKING OUT THE SPHERES TO BE RESEARCHED

In assessing the new problems posed by computerized archives, we have sought to clarify the choice of spheres to be researched within the Community in this connection.

It is appropriate to distinguish two aspects of the problems raised by the preservation and consultation of computerized archives: an intellectual aspect and a physical aspect.

5.2.1. The intellectual control of computerized archives

This relates to the actions to be carried out and the measures to be taken in particular in order to:

- ensure protection of the computerized archives (avoid their destruction, ensure that they are placed in the National Archives, guarantee their correct identification, etc.);
- ensure availability of the computerized archives (their access conditions etc.)

In this respect, although the objectives to be attained can be generally understood, significant divergences can be noted from one Member State to another concerning the methods of working used. Any action in this sphere must be subject:

- to a prior examination of the impact of information technology, particularly on present practices with regard to the creation of archives;
- to reflection on basic archival principles, such as the principle of source.

From their creation, computerized archives pose new questions for those who will later be responsible for their preservation and access.

These questions sometimes challenge well-established archival principles, such as the principle of source.

Firstly, what is the relationship between the social function of an institution, the new technology, the organizational structure and the information and statistics, and what is its impact on the formation of archives? In this respect the extent to which the use of computer techniques by the authorities influences the formation of archives constitutes an important aspect. [23]

The archive-producing organizations are currently making more and more use of the possibilities of exchanging information by electronic transmission, either between the departments and services of the same organization or between different organizations. It can be noted, however, that the integration of computers into vast networks linking various organizations is at present meeting the obstacle of a lack of standardization in these new automation applications. In other words, computerization of the archive-producing organizations is affecting their (i e the organizations') organizational structure:

---

[23] See Hedstrom, op. cit., pp. 344-345.

(i) firstly, the place of work is becoming more mobile. The growing automation of offices leads amongst other things to decentralized data storage;

(ii) secondly, whilst the large producers of archives traditionally apply the principle of division of labour, the new technologies involve other principles with regard to efficiency: within the same organization, the information systems are held more often in common between various departments and services.

These two factors (increased mobility and pooling of information within the same organization or between different organizations) make the author and origin of a document less identifiable. This is not to mention the corollary problem of dating the document.

On the other hand, does a clear line of demarcation exist in the case of some computerized archives between archives and documentation, and, if so, where is this drawn?[24] When the computerized archives are databases, the frontier between archives and documentation becomes indistinct: these documents are less static or more able to be manipulated.

Finally, what minimum criteria should be imposed upon the computerized archives at the time they are created, with regard to their identification? They are not always recorded files but often remain at the stage of potential connection between databases: such documents are only a collection of cross-references to other databases. In this case, the work of the archivist is complicated by the fact that he must not only save the databases but also the software and programmes which relate to them; he must also be aware of the possible applications and the procedures of making databases compatible. All these factors must form part of the analytical descriptions at the time of making inventories of computerized archives. These are in fáct data on data (meta-data) which must be mentioned to the user of computer archives. But it is at the time of their creation that the preservation of such data must be anticipated.

As can be seen, establishing the sources of computerized archives poses a major problem for archivists. Dictionaries of computer techniques are at the present time in preparation (IRDS — information resources dictionary standard). These will play an essential role in the future use of information systems. Under the aegis of the Community, the Member States and their experts could join forces in order to study the best methods of incorporating archival requirements into these dictionaries (particularly the maintenance of the principle of source).

Computerized archives, more than other media, make it imperative for the archivist to become involved in the formation of historical archives. More than ever, archivists must become involved at the time when documents are produced. Especially since those producing the archives pay little attention in general to the life cycle of the data. At the time of installing a new computer system, little consideration is given to the future management of the data, permanent preservation and file maintenance.

---

[24] See the 1990 ACCIS report, op. cit., pp. 21-24. The accent is placed here on the growing use of such communication methods in the decision-making process, which does not however give rise to the storage of the data.

On the other hand, with regard to access to computerized archives, in most of the Member States specific laws have been passed since the end of the 1970s which limit the computerization of data concerning people's private lives and which provide for control over the use of these facts.[25]

These laws relate in particular to: population registers, electoral registers, company registers, statistical information, credit risk registers (financial, banking, solvency information), road traffic registers, etc.

The preservation of computerized archives, which are under the jurisdiction of the National Archives, is more threatened than that of traditional archives by legislation relating to accessibility and by the practices of the authorities. Fear of computerization has created a strong current of political and bureaucratic opinion which leads to disastrous decisions if the situation is regarded from the point of view of research. Archivists have a role to play in the protection of this new form of collective memory. Without a specific law relating to the placing (in archives) and availability of banks of computer data, the legislation relating to personal data will apply. Thus this could lead to the destruction of information which, from an archival point of view, would merit preservation (see Annex 5).[26]

In what way could computer archives be made available to researchers? And, firstly, in what form? Could they be made available in a reading room in the form of a copy of a disk or other such? In any case, it is possible to take steps (through the locking of personal areas) to protect privacy: the National Archives could give confidentiality guarantees when they collect recent primary databases. The protection of copyright should also be taken into consideration in view of the specific nature of the medium.

Public inspection of computerized archives is still only exceptionally organized by the National Archives. The latter must ensure promotion of the use of their computerized archives.

Finally, a strictly practical question: it is more difficult to guarantee free access to computerized archives in view of the financial resources required. What will be the consequences of this for research?

---

[25] In France, the CNIL (National Committee of Computerization and Liberty), is responsible for controlling the application of information technology to the handling of personal data; it has decided that this information, as an exception from the provisions of the law relating to archives, is no longer available to the administration which produced it once it has been transferred to the National Archives.

[26] In Germany (Bundesarchiv) and in Denmark alone, legislation on archives takes a direct position on the transmission of computerized archives to the National Archives. In Denmark, the law on computerized registers stipulates that those records which contain information on individuals must be destroyed as soon as they have no further administrative use, unless there is special dispensation. But the new archive law provides for obligatory transfer to the National Archives of key registers from administrative archives, and facilitates the procedures of dispensation in order to obtain the preservation of other computerized registers of general significance. Access to computerized data is subject to prior agreement by the Registertilsyn (body supervising computerized public registers). When computerized data is transferred to the archives, this agreement is also required for all use, even when the applicant is the department having produced the data.

5.2.2. Physical control of computerized archives

Physical control of computerized archives is understood to mean all the actions to be taken and arrangements to be made in order to provide, and maintain, the data and the data media in their correct physical state, in order to resolve problems connected with reading computerized archives.

The National Archives must take into account a collection of measures designed to maintain the computerized archives' media in a good state of repair.[27] It is a question of guaranteeing durable physical preservation and the legibility of computerized archives in spite of the rapid technical development of the sector. Interest in Community action is considerable because:

- innovations with regard to information technology are important for everyone, particularly for archivists;
- research themes in this area are very concrete;
- there is less conflict of interests (particularly cultural conflict), given that the innovations are imposed from outside;
- significant financial interests are at stake.

A group of experts appointed by the Member States could research the most appropriate infrastructure for correct management of computerized archives, particularly with regard to storage and access and could recommend standards in this field.[28]

Archivists' concern regarding the ability to continue to identify a document in accordance with its source is in theory a concern which is shared by all those for whom the probationary and legal value of computerized documents is important. However, the role of archivists within standards organizations remains too unobtrusive. The standards in force at the present time (ODA/ODIF) remain insufficient.

The National Archives must ensure that as soon as a document is created, the administration sets its duration of preservation. They must also contribute to setting selection priorities for computerized archives.

---

[27] In France, computer databases from the departments of the central State administration are preserved and reformatted. In Germany, files are preserved in the archives in ASCII format in the form of regularly copied computer disks. In Denmark, in order to allow a preservation of data which is as independent as possible from contemporary techniques, computerized registers are transferred in the form of sequential files in ASCII format, with paper documentation of the connections between the data. In most of the Member States, it is the National Archives which decide the preservation standards of computerized documents (Belgium, Denmark, the United Kingdom). Elsewhere, decisions are taken in agreement with the departments having produced the data.

[28] Open systems, i.e. those whose databases and software can function without problems on hardware from different manufacturers, still have limited applications. In this area, an ISO pattern has existed since 1979 which allows for the creation of open communication systems, named OSI (open systems interconnection), built on seven levels. This model has been adopted as the national standard in the USA.

5.3. COLLABORATION PROJECTS

The information revolution already involves, to a greater or lesser degree, all the Member States of the Community. Hence all the Member States are confronted with the difficulties raised above. Are they going to handle them separately? If the answer is yes, there is a real risk of wasting much energy in the search for solutions which perhaps already exist elsewhere in the Community, whether it is a question of new working methods, standards, or of making sophisticated and expensive equipment available to the National Archives. Thus several arguments can be put forward in favour of a Community approach to the problem:

(a) this approach would make it easier to tackle problems than by one State in isolation, for example with regard to certain forms of research;

(b) a common approach has more weight in order to obtain from industry the application of technological standards, for example with regard to storage techniques or linguistic questions;

(c) an analysis by 12 is more efficient than 12 analyses;

(d) this approach allows a better guarantee of the quality of the solutions found.

It is appropriate, nevertheless, to examine the basis upon which a common approach to the management of computerized archives would have the best chance of success. This collaboration should not forget that policy for the management of computerized archives is settled by each Member State. Community research should begin by pooling the skills and knowledge present in the Community, by using recent statements on the question, such as the report of the working meeting on research issues in electronic records (Washington, 1991, p. 8) and the work of Hedstrom (op. cit., pp. 336 *et seq.*). It is from detailed comparative examination that solutions may arise.

Whilst the objective is to attain a general model of computerized archive management, particularly regarding storage, the pursuit of this objective implies:

- harmonization on a European level of the principles which govern the formation of archives;

- the setting of standards concerning the physical and logical preservation of computerized archives;

- research into substitution in view of the long-term management of and access to computerized archives;

- the choice of ideal standard infrastructures, taking into account the variety of problems which exist;

- if necessary, the creation of regulations, relating for example to the consultation of databases containing personal information.

51

5.4. DRAFT APPROACH FOR THE DEVELOPMENT OF JOINT PRINCIPLES RELATING TO THE MANAGEMENT OF COMPUTERIZED ARCHIVES

Prior to the preparation of a research programme, it would be appropriate to know the operations already used in the various Member States with regard to computerized archives. With this aim in mind, an inventory should be drawn up of research in progress, planned research and the results already acquired or awaited. It is important not to limit this inventory to the institutions which manage archives, but also to involve the governments (assuming that there is concern about this problem). The inventory will allow definition of Community research themes together with knowledge of the extent to which response has already been made and/or whether there are still gaps to be filled.

As soon as the research areas have been defined, the following decisions should be taken, independently of need:

(a) the research to be carried out per country, if possible within already existing initiatives which form the object of coordination, in order to avoid duplication; agreements relating to the exchange of research results (for example, in the form of publications, symposiums, etc.);

(b) the creation of a Community research programme.

This Community research programme will without doubt have more success in finding immediate applications in the field of physical control of computerized archives since, as noted, there are fewer conflicts of interests in this area.

CHAPTER 6

THE EXCHANGE OF ARCHIVAL INFORMATION AND COMPUTER NETWORKS BETWEEN THE MEMBER STATES

By introducing more generalized automation, the tasks of archivists can be facilitated at the same time as offering more extensive services to the users.

With the aid of current technology it should also be possible to create compatible systems of archival information and integrate these within national and eventually European networks.

Exchanges of databases can also be carried out by means of CD-ROM publishing.

In this sphere, archives have to fill an evident gap in comparison with other information sectors.

Whilst awaiting a European network of information exchange specific to archives, it would be appropriate at the present time to undertake joint action between Member States in identifying and accepting computer standards which would be of the most interest for the archival world.

In any case, any new initiative will only be able to refer to attainments already made on a national level, by encouraging their coordination of these and particularly by recommending the use of open systems. It will be necessary at the same time to seek an agreement for researching and promoting archival description standards.

A working party could be made responsible for drawing up short- and long-term plans in this area, having firstly to make an inventory of existing computer applications in the National Archives and then to promote research into descriptive standards specific to archives. This would have the aim of bringing information technology into widespread use with regard to the processing of archival information and facilitating dissemination of the latter through the creation of national and then European networks, with Community support.

In agreement with the Resolution of 14 November 1991, which stated that archives were an essential tool for writing history and defining the cultural identity of Europe and of its Member States, and taking into account the common history of the said Member States, it appears highly desirable to establish an automated system of information exchange between the archive repositories of the various Member States. This network should permit remote access to the information contained in the archives through various means.

6.1. COMPUTERIZATION OF ARCHIVES IN THE MEMBER STATES

Over the last few years, archive work in Europe, as in the rest of the world, has been influenced by developments in information technology. Institutions, both public and private, are producing documents in non-traditional forms with their own special characteristics; this has implications both for legislation and for archival working methods.

However, in most countries the main impact of new technology has been in the use of new computerized tools for improving document management and conservation and the dissemination of information.

There has been a spectacular increase in the use of these new tools for archive work, especially since the arrival of microcomputers; rapidly falling prices and the growing availability of user-friendly software have made computers accessible even to the non-specialist.

In fact, the variety of computer applications now utilized by archivists is such that many of the advantages of the new technology have been nullified. Moreover, many of these tools are fairly limited, being used simply to computerize tasks previously performed manually (replacement of traditional files by computerized information retrieval systems, or database management systems).

With a few exceptions, there has been little progress in creating systems for the large-scale dissemination or exchange of archival information in electronic form or through information networks, and since archivists have shown little interest in developing open systems it is hardly surprising that those projects that have been carried out are incompatible.

In recent years, many countries have therefore changed their approach to preparing general plans for computerizing national archives. However, with the exception of the contacts that take place in international organizations (International Council on Archives, Unesco, etc.), there is no evidence of any desire among the EU Member States to coordinate their efforts.

6.2. NEW TECHNOLOGY — WHAT DOES IT OFFER?

The importance of modernizing archival information systems by using computer technology is by now self-evident. Many tasks can be carried out more easily and more effectively with the assistance of computers. The new technology can even be used to set up unified archival information systems which can incorporate all the descriptive information contained in other formats, allowing multiple forms of access and facilitating at the same time ways of obtaining direct access to information while respecting the principle of ownership.

One of the main functions of archives is to disseminate information and it is here that the new technology offers many advantages by giving quicker, more efficient and more decentralized access to information.

At the most basic level, word-processing systems can greatly facilitate traditional description work. Information retrieval systems, database management systems, hypertext, and so on, are all tools for creating archive management systems and archival information systems which will be even further improved by applying the techniques of artificial intelligence (and expert systems in particular).

Digital sound and vision technology, multimedia systems and new data media — mainly optical — all have the potential to help conserve documents and disseminate the information they contain.

Finally, ever more powerful and complex communications networks offering remote access to information or electronic data exchange, not to mention the tremendous potential of electronic publishing using today's CD-ROM technology, will all help bring about the decentralized utilization of vast amounts of data.

6.3. REMOTE ACCESS TO INFORMATION

6.3.1. Current developments in telecommunications are speeding up the 'global village' process by eliminating geographical barriers to the spread of information and promoting links between different information resources through the use of increasingly powerful networks so that information, storage capacity and computer applications can be shared and exploited.

Basic telephone networks (public switched telephone network — PSTN) exist in all countries, providing the infrastructure for any kind of information transmission. These are usually complemented by networks specifically designed for information management and exchange (the so-called packet switched data network — PSDN), both public and private: all the countries in the European Union have at least one public data transmission network, based on the CCITT's X.25 standard in addition to other standards for linking up separate networks (such as X.75), or for accessing the PSDN via the PSTN (such as X.28 or X.32).

However, these networks are still limited to transmitting certain types of information or small quantities of data; the capacity and speed at which they operate prevent them, for example, from sending high-quality digital images of archive documents. This constraint will be removed by new developments (fibre optics in particular) which will allow the introduction of the new integrated services data networks (ISDN), or universal networks, that will be able to offer all kinds of public service on one network: improved telephony, teletext, telefax, teleconference facilities, videotext, high-quality television, interactive television, intercomputer communications, multimedia databases, etc. The Community has given full backing to the setting-up of a European ISDN, although it is far from being at the same stage of development in every Member State.

6.3.2. A number of institutions interested in the exchange of scientific information are using this basic communications infrastructure to set up information exchange networks. The computer resources of the institutions participating in the network are made available to authorized users (with open or restricted access) who may or may not have to pay for them. National academic networks link up universities and research centres and connect them up with the rest of the world. It is possible, for example, to use the Spanish IRIS network to gain on-line access to the large databases available on international networks such as Internet which allow remote access to information from anywhere in the world.

But access to information is not the whole story; other services such as teleconferencing or electronic mail are available to users of these networks, although it is true that the most popular service is accessing ASCII databases.

One particular type of network centralizes information from all the institutions making up the network in a single central computer which controls, manages, stores and distributes all information. One such example is the research library information network (RLIN) which was set up by the Research Library Group (RLG) and based in the central computer of Stanford University, California.

One advantage of these centralized networks for libraries which does not apply to archives is that each book only has to be catalogued once even if it is held by every single library in the network, since each centre incorporates into the basic catalogue details of all the volumes on its shelves: this system greatly facilitates the production of collective catalogues and other services such as interlibrary lending. However, it only works with very precise description standards (AACR2) and information exchange formats (MARC).

6.3.3. All these forms of information exchange have been made possible by the generalized use of certain technical standards. Some of the many standards issued by various bodies have been mentioned above; these all have to comply with the ISO's 1979 general standard (ISO 7498) on setting up open communication systems through the open systems interconnection (OSI) reference model which regulates the exchange of information between networks and the systems created by various manufacturers.

The OSI model establishes seven levels of communication: from the physical level (Level 1), which controls the physical connection between the networks, to the applications level (Level 7) which provides the means of communication for the user's applications programmes. Each level uses the services provided by lower levels and at the same time provides services to higher levels. These standards allow different systems to communicate, filtering data sent by one system so that it is intelligible to the system receiving it.

Alongside the OSI reference model levels, there are other standards drawn up by different bodies which are used by hardware and software producers to eliminate information compatibility problems. As far as the exchange of archival information is concerned, it is those standards which relate to the top two levels (presentation and application) that are of most interest: ODA/ODIF, FTAM, DTAM, etc.

Another advantage for archives, in addition to facilitating exchanges of information, will be the ability to switch to new systems to bypass the problems of obsolescence and the long-term conservation of information, and to reduce dependency on hardware and software manufacturers to a minimum.

In any case, the OSI reference model provides a basis for standardizing information exchanges, although it does not influence the individual programmes chosen by each user nor of course does it affect the purely archival work, such as description, that was carried out before any databases were set up. There are no generally accepted norms for programmes for computerizing archival tasks such as, for example, reading room control or description methods, or for setting up databases containing archival information.

6.3.4. Apart from some experiments in international data exchange, only a few national projects have so far been carried out in Europe.

Any project will in any event have to take account of existing standards, especially those relating specifically to archival work (for example, description standards, so as to make the best use of any databases set up).

6.3.5. The European Union is undertaking various activities in the field of remote access to databases under Impact, Comett, ECHO, etc. For example, the multilingual interrogation mock-up (MIM) is an attempt at solving one of the most difficult problems faced by the member countries, namely the number of different languages.

Any work undertaken in this area by a group such as the group of experts on archives should take these projects and all relevant guidelines into account.

6.4. REMOTE ACCESS AND CD-ROM

Since the arrival of new electronic publishing systems using optical media, remote access to databases is no longer the only option — thanks to CD-ROM technology, databases can now be accessed directly using any personal computer.

Because a single CD-ROM contains such a large quantity of data, is reasonably inexpensive, and is easy to consult directly by anybody with a personal computer, a new editorial industry exploiting optical media has grown up and now offers a feasible alternative to traditional forms of on-line inquiry. Indeed, the European Union itself now offers some of its databases such as CELEX, its Community law database, in a CD-ROM version.

Both methods will probably continue to coexist in the future, each one with its own advantages and disadvantages:

- for intensive use, CD-ROM is cheaper than on-line searching;
- CD-ROM user interfaces are generally much simpler;
- on-line searching has the edge if databases are updated frequently.

6.5. LINES OF ACTION

A European network for exchanging archival information is still some way off at present. Nevertheless, some guidelines and measures can even now be suggested.

(a) Identify standards affecting the exchange of information in the future.

(b) Inform archivists of these standards and recommend their use.

(c) Undertake a detailed inventory and analysis of computer applications currently used in European State archives and their potential for the exchange of information.

(d) Using as a basis existing standards for setting up open systems, start work on creating a minimum standardization framework for such applications.

(e) With a view to introducing general standards for archive management, seek an agreement on the use of archival description standards based on the work of the ICA/Unesco *ad hoc* Commission on Descriptive Standards.

(f) Promote the creation of databases containing archival information in accordance with these guidelines so that they form the first links in a future archive exchange network.

(g) Ensure that plans for archive exchange are in harmony with information exchange projects backed by the Community in other areas (bibliographic and museum information, etc.) while respecting the specific characteristics of archival information.

(h) Set up a working party with the task of drawing up short- and long-term plans, making practical project proposals and defining priorities.

(The Spanish experiment with computerized networks is presented in Annex 6.)

CHAPTER 7

THE TRAINING OF ARCHIVISTS AND RECOGNITION OF DIPLOMAS

A revaluation of the role of archivists, regardless of their level of training, should be based on the adaptation of their training to the requirements of contemporary archival practices and on a better valuation of the specific nature of this training compared with other information sciences.

This revaluation should also be based on official recognition of the title of archivist. To achieve this, it seems important at the outset to discuss, on a European scale, the diplomas and the national syllabuses upon which these diplomas are based. Secondly, the national syllabuses could form the subject of dialogue, cooperation and multilateral or European exchanges. The dialogue could go as far as the mutual recognition of diplomas, as encouraged by the Council Directives of 21 December 1988 and 18 June 1992.

Even before having reached this mutual recognition of diplomas, the training of archivists would certainly benefit from a networking of the various establishments and archive training centres: advantage could then be taken of the complementary nature of the training given in Europe in order to offer more specialized courses and seminars. Economies of scale could also be achieved in the in-service training and the organization of seminars, access to which could be reserved as a priority for young archivists.

The European institutions could be a driving force in the sphere of in-service training, by allowing the archive training establishments and centres to benefit from programmes such as Erasmus, Tempus or Lingua, which reinforce interuniversity cooperation through mobility grants, and by contributing to the organization of European seminars designed for specialists in one or another archival discipline.

7.1. ONE PROBLEM ON THE AGENDA

The archivist's job has changed more in one generation than since its distant origins. Its institutional, economic and technological environment is developing rapidly and the archivist must incessantly adapt to this changing context. The construction of Europe will accelerate the process of change in this part of the world. The management of archives has changed considerably in the information society which has come into existence at the end of the 20th century and of which the service sector is one of the most tangible signs.

In the sphere of training archivists, as in nearly all other spheres connected with this profession, the flow of international information exchange has grown considerably in latter years.

The International Council on Archives has recently held two conferences on this theme, in Paris in 1988 and in Milan in 1989, initiated by its Committee on Professional Training. These conferences coincided with the publication by the periodical *Archivum* of a special edition devoted to the professional training of archivists.

At Marburg, in 1989, before confirming the profound changes in the German syllabuses, the heads of the main European training establishments were invited to give their own points of view, over two days, concerning the multiple reforms in management. This meeting gave the opportunity for preparing an updated vision of the state of the art in Europe.[29]

In 1990, in Lyons, the 31st Congress of French archivists, relating to European integration, raised in particular the question of harmonization of training amongst the Member States. This came up against various obstacles (language, administrative traditions, both intellectual and academic), but comparisons could be drawn between the various systems in existence in an attempt to take the richer and stronger national elements and adapt them elsewhere.

Finally, at the conference organized in Maastricht in 1991 by the Association of Dutch Archivists, the theme of which was 'Archives in a Europe without frontiers', some 15 of the 65 papers presented related to the training of the archivist in Europe and requested a follow-up in this sphere.

7.2. TRAINING LEVELS

The archive training establishments and centres in Europe have a rich history, the older ones dating back to the beginning of the 19th century. The EU Member States today have a growing number of establishments which organize appropriate training for future archivists.

There are at least two levels of archivist training; some Member States such as France have even more.

Firstly there is specialized university training, entered after obtaining a diploma in a general field; this type of training spread after the Second World War.

Alternatively, since the status of archivists working in the public archives is generally that of official, there are numerous specialized institutes which only give instruction on archives. They are often set up in or near archive repositories. In Italy, schools of diplomatic and archival palaeography are established near archive repositories in the regional towns.

---

[29] Eckhardt, W. A., Wissenschaftliche Archivarsausbildung in Europa, Veröffentlichungen der Archivarschule Marburg — Institut für Archivwissenschaft, Marburger Vorträge, No 14, Marburg 1989.

In Spain, candidates can study at university (Master of Archives) or at specialized institutes called 'Escuelas-Taller de Archivos'.

The conditions of entry to the training courses offered vary considerably from one Member State to another. In most cases, a university education or equivalent is formally required for entering either a specialized or a postgraduate school (specialization of an academic kind).

In France, entry to the highest functions (conservateur) in the central civil service is reserved to archivists-palaeographers. They have received training at L'École des Chartes (two years' preparation, three years' school) supplemented by a period of 18 months at L'École nationale du Patrimoine. Although these studies do not formally confer a university title, the archivist-palaeographer's diploma can be taken there.

In the United Kingdom, archive administration courses appear on the course programmes of four universities and, in addition, the Society of Archivists organizes a correspondence course.

Whilst it is not absolutely necessary to be a historian before entering archivist training, it is noted that in most of the Member States, historians are the most numerous amongst those specializing in this field. Germany, Belgium and France stress the importance of the archivist's education in history at university level and in any case recruit the largest number of their archival officials from amongst those holding degrees in history.

The level of the diplomas and the duration of study necessary for obtaining the diploma of archivist vary considerably (from some weeks to several years). In Germany (at the Schools of Marburg, Munich and Potsdam), the Netherlands and Portugal, for example, two levels of archivist training exist which relate to two different types of employment: academic duties and non-academic duties.

In order to enter the non-university training, it is necessary to have a diploma in studies at the level of A level (England), the baccalaureate (France).

As a result of this, the term 'archivist' has different meanings both within one Member State and from one Member State to another. Archivists are trained in accordance with procedures which lead to variable levels of qualification.

In order to attempt to respond to the new constraints, to which we will return when speaking of the syllabuses, it appears appropriate that the establishments which give archival training should coordinate their activities, particularly with regard to allowing easier entry to students from other Member States, in order to facilitate the eventual international mobility of public and private archivists. These institutions could usefully be put into a network. They would become open and interdependent partners on a Community level. They would thus take part in a vast clearing-house.

At the present time, however, the various training courses given within one Member State are still not coordinated, and encouraging dialogue between the various branches in one Member State would be a first step.

In Italy, the 17 establishments giving archival training courses which are set up near the State Archives can be considered, apart from the common basis of their courses, which is national, to be an expression of the tendency towards a greater decentralization of training.

In the near future, the European institutions could play a leading role by placing archivists within courses such as Erasmus, Tempus or Lingua,[30] which encourage interuniversity cooperation by mobility grants.

7.3. ARCHIVIST TRAINING COURSES

Existing archivist training courses have been made the object of several comprehensive studies on a European level. These give prominence to the recent efforts on the part of several Member States to make these courses more appropriate to present archival practices:

(a) the considerable increase in the volume of archives and thus the necessity of training the future archivist to respond to these numerous tasks and to his significant responsibility, particularly with regard to sorting and disposal;

(b) the difficulties experienced by numerous authorities and other producers of archives in managing current, medium-term and historical archives; the archivist is called upon more and more to manage archives throughout their life cycle at the same time as offering the users the sources available;

(c) the growing necessity of responding quickly to questions which necessitate a command of the information contained in the archives; the archivist is more and more judged on his capacity to develop new and efficient research tools;

(d) the necessity of mastering information technology, on the one hand, because of the appearance of new types of archives and, on the other hand, because of the necessity to make archive access easier.

In several Member States, the updating of the syllabuses is the result of collaboration between the professional archivists associations and the specialized schools or universities which give training. In the United Kingdom, the professional association periodically re-examines the content of training courses which apply for recognition.

The adaption of syllabuses must be made around the three basic features of any archival training:

(i) a knowledge of present and past government, its organization and its development;

(ii) the practice of historical research and a knowledge of the sciences related to history, in such a way as to be able to consider history over a long period and to manage the memory of communities and institutions: immediate memory or

---

[30] Lingua: programme to promote the teaching and learning of foreign languages in the European Community.
Erasmus: European Community action scheme for the mobility of university students.
Tempus: Trans-European mobility scheme for university studies.
Comett: Community action programme in education and training for technology.

62

permanent memory; to be able also to assist users, to help them regarding the possible choices of research subjects as well as regarding the documents to be used at the time of this research;

(iii) the study of archives and the methods of processing information. The information sciences call for specific approaches and tools which the archivist must master unless he wants his role taken over by other information specialists.

It is precisely because his function combines these three main axes that the archivist has to receive specific training.

It should be noted in addition that a knowledge of several languages, at the time of information application worldwide and the opening of Europe's internal frontiers, is a considerable advantage.

Teaching already combines theory and practice everywhere in Europe. Practising archivists must be able to pass on their know-how through methodological accounts as well as practical exercises, which will be more profitable when carried out *in situ*, i.e. in the archive-producing authorities and in the archive services near to these authorities.

The history, language, culture and legislation of the various Member States differentiate them too much to be able to envisage extensive harmonization of archival training. All the work carried out at the present time on the question nevertheless emphasizes that the development of syllabuses should henceforth concentrate on the common foundation of professional knowledge upon which the profession of archivist is based.

The career of archivist will retain its specific features if the necessary development and revaluation of the archivist role is carried out in the face of the recent developments in modern technology which are increasingly affecting and changing its sphere.

7.4. THE MUTUAL RECOGNITION OF DIPLOMAS

The mutual recognition of legislation and diplomas is a consequence of the networking of existing training.

The question of training archivists in Europe is connected with related problems, such as that of the recognition of higher education diplomas within the Community. Council Directive 89/48/EEC of 21 December 1988 stipulates that:

'when, in a host Member State, the taking up or pursuit of a regulated profession is subject to the possession of a diploma, the competent authority may not, on the grounds of inadequate qualification, refuse to authorize a national of a Member State to take up or pursue that profession on the same conditions as its nationals, if the applicant holds the diploma required by another Member State for the taking up or pursuit of the profession in question or if the applicant has pursued the profession in question full-time for two years during the previous 10 years'.

Council Directive 92/51/EEC of 18 June 1992 relating to a second general system for the recognition of professional training supplements Directive 89/48/EEC.

In effect this new legislation leaves the host Member State the option of submitting the candidate to an aptitude test or to a probationary period of a limited duration. In this way it can be left to the Member States to recruit archivists on the basis of a higher education diploma or other certificates relating to specific knowledge (language of the host country, history-connected sciences and others).

In order to facilitate the mutual recognition of diplomas, it could be proposed that the various Member States adopt minimum criteria recognized by all, which would regulate entry into the profession of archivist:

(i) possession of a university degree or equivalent diploma, issued after at least four years of university study;

(ii) an in-depth knowledge of national history, particularly of institutional history; an elementary knowledge of law and of the sources of national law, of archives and of information technology; an in-depth knowledge of the language of the country.

In several Member States, the profession of archivist is not subject to the possession of a diploma in archival studies.

In order to emphasize the particular nature of the profession of archivist, Member States should be encouraged to set up both training programmes leading to the obtaining of a recognized diploma and courses in specifically archival skills.

With particular reference to archivists working for the National Archives, it is a matter for each Member State to reserve certain administrative responsibilities to its nationals, but these reservations should remain exceptions. This implies the revision of certain provisions of the civil service law, which reserves entry to some parts to nationals alone. The international mobility of archivists would be facilitated by legal and statutory provisions established by each Member State.

7.5. SPECIALIZATION

A common-core teaching syllabus for archivists remains indispensable. Nevertheless, the progressive networking of the various establishments and training centres would allow, in some cases, archivists to specialize from the beginning of their training.

In the case of National Archives, specialization of the members of the staff can prove useful if there are large numbers. It can be useful to give separate training:

(i) according to the age of the documents for which the archivist will be responsible; it is necessary in this connection to take account of the growing need for archivists capable of handling large quantities of contemporary archives;

(ii) in accordance with the type of collection and the diversity of the archive producers; this would allow, for example, the training of archivists specialized in company archives;

(iii) in accordance with the various media of the documents (thinking obviously of the preservation of computerized documents).

On the other hand, the training of the personnel specifically involved with the material preservation of the documents could, perhaps, more easily be made the object of coordination on a European scale, since the problems encountered in this sphere are the same everywhere.

7.6. TRAINING AT THE BEGINNING OF THE ARCHIVIST'S CAREER IN THE NATIONAL ARCHIVES

The training received at the beginning of a career in archives is more often than not limited to a training period without structured training: six months in Spain, two years in the United Kingdom, and 18 months of École d'Application after the École des Chartes in France. In Italy, the State Archives organize a two-year course ending in an examination for archivist candidates.

Prospective Belgian archivists follow the courses of the 'Rijksarchiefschool' in The Hague or the International Training Course on Archives in Paris. Their training period, of at least two years, leads to an assessment made by the same examiners who recruited them.

In Denmark, the National Archives stipulate professional training of two and a half years after recruitment. The training consists of a continuous series of practical courses, which can be supplemented by additional studies if the student so wishes. It ends with an evaluation of qualifications.

Several Member States already emphasize the interest they would have in the idea of those responsible for national training letting one another know of their training syllabuses and meeting regularly in order to introduce practical forms of cooperation.

7.7. IN-SERVICE TRAINING

7.7.1. In-service training within the Member States

The subjects covered in in-service training courses (seminars) generally place emphasis on the management qualities of the archivist, new methods used within the profession, the handling of new archives and in general all the areas of archival study within which problems develop quickly and extensively. In several Member States in-service training is still not organized.

This in-service training is particularly aimed at young archivists. Its effectiveness is greatest when it lasts for one or two weeks, based around a given theme and balancing methodology and practical exercises.

7.7.2. International exchanges of archivists between National Archives

Exchanges of information and of people between the National Archives of the Member States already exist but they should be encouraged and developed. At this time, relationships between the various Member States' training establishments exist but are not highly developed. By way of example, there are some experiments which should be mentioned. Since 1951, the international technical training course in archives which takes place each year in Paris has allowed young archivists to compare their experiences and has given them the opportunity to make contact with colleagues from other continents. It should be emphasized that this international technical training course is aimed ideally at archivists already having an in-depth knowledge of archives.

Dutch-speaking archivists from Belgium follow courses at the Rijksarchiefschool in The Hague with their Dutch opposite numbers. For its part, the European Commission actively collaborates with the National Archives of Belgium and Luxembourg in organizing courses intended for archivists connected with the secretariates, the Directorates-General and Commission departments.

Short seminars are perhaps the most effective: it is not necessary to become immersed in the life of a country for months in order to become initiated into its professional practices, but short periods abroad, as when taking part in international meetings, enlarge archivists' horizons. It is particularly appropriate to seek to form contacts with neighbouring countries for obvious historical reasons: economic, political and cultural contacts are naturally deeper between neighbouring countries.

7.7.3. European seminars designed for specialists

In addition to the in-service training which is open to all archivists, archival seminars intended for specialists could be organized on a European level.

Themes which could be used for the period 1993-95 are: basic ideas of terminology, review at institutional level, access to archives, preservation and conservation, the applications of information technology to archives, service to the public, freedom of movement of cultural goods and standardization of the tools of research.

Regardless of the place where these European seminars are organized, the organizing institutions must have the necessary budget and infrastructure (in premises, audiovisual and computer equipment, etc.). In addition, these seminars are even more beneficial when they provide knowledge about archives which are still current or medium-term. In other words, they should be held near institutions which produce archives.

7.8. PROJECTS AND RECOMMENDATIONS

In conclusion, it seems possible to extract some main themes for future action regarding training. In this sphere it should be possible to:

(a) encourage in all ways recognition of the specific nature of archivist training in comparison with other information specialists, particularly by incorporating these specificities within the training school syllabuses;

(b) encourage official recognition of the title of archivist by the various Member States, by recognizing diplomas and defining the syllabuses relating to these diplomas;

(c) encourage Member States to set up specific training courses where they do not already exist and appear to be necessary;

(d) further all forms of joint activity, cooperation and multilateral or European exchanges between the various establishments and centres which give specific archivist training. This cooperation should eventually lead to networking the schools;

(e) study possibilities of furthering mutual recognition of diplomas between Member States;

(f) work on in-service training of archivists, particularly young archivists, by allowing them to benefit from European programmes such as Erasmus, Tempus, Lingua, etc., and by organizing European seminars, specifically destined for specialists in various archival disciplines.

CHAPTER 8
PRIVATE ARCHIVES

Although national legislation determines different types of documents as being private archives, the objectives of the supervision of private archives are to ensure that these documents are preserved and can be consulted.

One of the measures specifically recommended by the experts is at least to increase the inventories of private archives, particularly on the grounds of the EU regulations relating to the export of cultural goods and the return of cultural goods which have been unlawfully removed from the territory of a Member State.

Several Member States prepare inventories of private archives, taking into account their significance for the history and culture of the States concerned and also for their national identity.

It is necessary for the movement of these archives to be controlled, by promoting instead the circulation of the information which they contain (distribution of lists of known contents, copying, exchanges by computer networks, etc.).

The experts draw attention, on the other hand, to the necessity of seeking active collaboration with the donors, holders or owners of private archives (including company archives) and of providing various incentives, even using taxation, to encourage them to keep them where they are, to ensure their preservation and to facilitate access to them under the right conditions.

Following the opening of the single market, the Council and the Commission issued a Directive and two Regulations concerning the free movement of cultural goods. Included in cultural goods are archives of all kinds containing elements which are more than 50 years old, regardless of their media.

These texts already demonstrate the existence of an explicit concern on the part of the Community with regard to safeguarding and protecting private archives as an important part of archival heritage. The application of the measures in question implies the organization of cooperation between the Member States.

Finally, the National Archives should seek collaboration of all kinds (human, scientific and material) with the associations and research centres which, in each Member State, act on behalf of the preservation and use of private archives. The Community could serve as a framework for operational meetings and for the development of draft agreements in this area.

The observations contained in this report are based on two principal considerations:

(1) The expression 'private archives' generally covers a rather vast documentary typology, still not precisely defined by various national legislations and which can vary widely from one Member State to another.

(2) The deadline of 1 January 1993 has made the problem relating to the preservation and use of such archives even more immediate, since, as a result of their intrinsic nature, they seem more easily subject to movement and to unlawful export.

From another point of view, it is undeniable that private archives, in the same way as public archives, constitute an important source of the history of numerous countries, particularly the European countries. However, the State supervision of private archives, which will be discussed later, can vary from one country to another, since it relates as much to a definition of the law of ownership as to the various typologies which such archives can constitute.

Attention is consequently focused on some points which are considered to be fundamental to the complex process of State supervision of private archives. Profound thought on these points is considered to be necessary, particularly with a view to the possible creation of common structures.

In writing the report, account has been taken of the comparative examination and summarized schedule of national legislation on this matter, compiled by A. Ducrot, 'Archives personnelles et familiales — Statut légal et problèmes juridiques', in *La Gazette des Archives*, No 157, July 1992. In addition, reference will often be made to Italian experience, given that it is based on a rather broad concept of State supervision.

8.1. DEFINITION OF PRIVATE ARCHIVES

Generally speaking, archives which are not public are considered to be private. However, national legislation can determine as private very different documentary typologies.

In Italy, for example, the archives of various public authorities which do not have territory as a constituent element (some universities, banks, hospitals and cultural institutes) are public, whereas in the United Kingdom the universities and the banks are considered to be private.

In Italy the definition of private archives makes reference to documentary collections of various kinds: family archives or those of individual persons, trades unions, (political) parties, cultural institutes, associations, foundations, enterprises, credit institutions and agencies, whereas ecclesiastical archives are only similar to private archives.

The heterogeneous nature of the typologies results in different ways of exercising supervision.

8.2. SUPERVISION PROJECT FOR PRIVATE ARCHIVES

The main aim of a correctly applied protection operation is to guarantee that documentary collections are preserved in such a way that their consultation is allowed. Thus a policy could be pursued which would lead to minimum objectives: a good state of preservation, united and intact collections, the possibility of access, the existence of research tools (lists, catalogues, inventories) to facilitate consultation. More incisive supervision should, on the other hand, allow the possibility of photocopying or microfilming sets and collections and the creation of a computerized network which would allow data access and exchange.

8.2.1. Bodies responsible for supervision and their regulations

In this respect, national legislation is very divergent: in some Member States no supervisory body is provided, while in others, although it is provided for by law, it is not in fact set up.

In Italy, the supervision of private archives is carried out by the Sovrintendenze Archivistiche (these number 20 and are based in the main towns of each region). The instrument which the law makes available to them is the 'dichiarazione di notevole interesse storico', an administrative standard by means of which the historical significance of a documentary collection or individual documents (and thus public interest in the preservation of these documents) can be established. Certain obligations for the private owner, possessor or holder derive from this historical significance.

In France on the other hand provision is made for classification as historical archives and this is a measure which can be taken either administratively or with the agreement of the private holder. The obligations which derive from this classification are less onerous than those provided for by Italian law.

In the United Kingdom, the responsibility for taking an inventory of private archives is given to the Royal Commission on Historical Manuscripts, which also has responsibility for advising the owners or holders and setting the criteria for drawing up inventories and possibly publishing them.

8.2.2. Obligations for the owner

In this case also, the standards emanating from the various Member States are very diverse: some stipulate no obligations at all for the owner (the Netherlands), while others stipulate differentiated obligations.

Italian law is perhaps the most strict in this respect, at least in principle: the private owner must in effect take care to preserve the archives or individual documents by ordering them, drawing up an inventory and restoring them, whether he carries this out himself or consents to the State carrying it out; he must allow consultation, upon which he can place limits in accordance with the private nature of certain documents; he cannot dismember the archives, or sell or export them without prior authorization by the Sovrintendenza. It must, however, be emphasized that Italian legislation does not stipulate sanctions for those private owners who do not respect these provisions, with the exception of enforced placing (of the archives) in the Archivio di Stato which has jurisdiction over the territory: this can constitute, in more serious cases, a considerable obstacle to protecting private archives.

8.2.3. Incentives to the owners or holders of private archives

The importance of supervision which is based upon collaboration with the private owners is now widely acknowledged; in the same way it is noted that good results are obtained by a policy of persuasion. From this viewpoint, many Member States have resorted to tax relief, for example the United Kingdom, France and Italy (Law 512/82). In Italy provision is also made for a grant, by the State, of financial contributions for the preservation of private archives which are declared to be of considerable historical interest (Law 253/86).

8.2.4. Supervision by acquisition

The States can also carry out supervision of private archives by acquiring those which are no longer subject to risk. This acquisition can be made in different ways (purchase, donation, legacy, transfer), stipulated by legislation or practised informally in several Member States (the United Kingdom, the Netherlands, France, Italy, Spain, Germany, Belgium).

In Italy, private owners have the possibility of placing their archives temporarily with preservation institutions run by the State, but there is nothing to prevent them from placing them with other public or private institutions (cultural institutes, local authorities, etc.).

Although such placing constitutes a revocable contract, national legislation is very divergent with regard to its minimum duration (10 years in Portugal and the Netherlands, 99 years in Belgium; in Italy no limit is stipulated, given that the contract is always subject to the wishes of the private owner).

8.2.5. Access to private archives

It has already been stated that one of the objectives of supervision is to allow the consultation of private archives. This can constitute an obligation for the owner, as provided for by Italian law, but the best solution seems to be to that of making at least descriptive lists of the collections available. It cannot, however, be denied that whilst on the one hand such a solution is appropriate for researchers, it could cause some apprehension to the owners. This seems to us to be one of the cases where the interests of the State and the necessities of research are more difficult to reconcile with the interests of the private owner.

8.2.6. Supervision of sales of private archives

The discovery on the open market of private documentary antiquities of historical significance is far from being rare. Control of this sphere is rather difficult. Italian law provides for the exercise of a right of pre-emption in the case of archives being sold; however, the 'Sovrintendenze' are not always alerted in time to be able to exercise this pre-emption. The main difficulty seems therefore to relate to the fact that there is no knowledge of the sale until long afterwards.

A right of pre-emption is also provided for by, amongst others, Portuguese and Spanish legislation. It is not provided, on the other hand, by the legislation of Germany, Belgium or the United Kingdom.

8.2.7. Supervision of the export of private archives

With regard to this aspect, it can be noted that some countries are very liberal (northern Europe in general), whilst others are very protectionist (southern Europe).

Similar legal regimes can however relate to different realities; prior authorization by the competent authorities is, however, provided for in nearly all countries.

It is nevertheless desirable that, with the opening of the single market, some of the problems in this area be resolved in the light of the European standard in the matter.

Following the opening of the single market, the Council and the Commission issued a Directive as well as two Regulations concerning the free movement of cultural goods. These included archives of all kinds comprising elements more than 50 years old in 'cultural goods', regardless of their medium.[31]

---

[31] Council Regulation (EEC) No 3911/92 of 9 December 1992 relating to the export of cultural goods (OJ L 395, 31.12.1992, pp. 1-3).
Council Directive 93/7/EEC of 15 March 1993 relating to the return of cultural goods having been unlawfully removed from the territory of a Member State (OJ L 74, 27.3.1993, pp. 74-80).
Commission Regulation (EEC) No 752/93 of 30 March 1993, relating to application provisions for Council Regulation (EEC) No 3911/92 relating to the export of cultural goods (OJ L 77, 31.3.1993, pp. 24-26).

8.2.8. Private current archives of historical interest

A completely specific problem is that of current archives (archives under formation), which exist in nearly all the typologies referred to above (8.1). In Italy, although the law provides for the possibility of declaring such archives to be of considerable historical interest, intervention by the supervisory bodies is always rather difficult, and this constitutes an obstacle to protecting this part of future national heritage.

8.3. CONCLUSIONS

In the light of what has been stated above, it is appropriate to give some advice regarding the better protection of private archives:

8.3.1. to increase the inventories of existing private archives in the various Member States;

8.3.2. to disseminate a maximum amount of information relating to those archives which are recognized as having significance for national history, if possible by using a computer network;

8.3.3. to set up or develop a system of exchanges by microfilming documents which may also be relevant to the history of a country other than that of the place of preservation;

8.3.4. to institute a policy of tax relief in order to prevent the 'escape' or unjustified movement of private archives;

8.3.5. to provide a system which sanctions the violation of standards relating to the movement of archives in Europe;

8.3.6. to promote adequate valuation campaigns relating to the private documentary heritage in order to make the owners aware of the need for suitable preservation of this heritage;

8.3.7. to encourage all forms of collaboration between the National Archives and the research associations and centres which could lead to actions of protection and valuation with respect to the private archive heritage.

CHAPTER 9

THE COMMUNITY ARCHIVES

Two legal instruments were adopted in 1983 by the Council and the Commission, opening the Community archives (those of the ECSC and of the EEC and Euratom) to the public under the 30-year rule. The texts (a Regulation and a Decision) had been jointly agreed and prepared by the Member States and the institutions. Cooperation, though, did not stop there — for example, the archive services of the Ministries of Foreign Affairs and those of the institutions together published a guide in 1989 designed to facilitate access to Community archives. In addition, the institutions agreed to deposit the originals of archives opened to the public with the European University Institute in Florence (EUIF) — itself an active centre of historical research.

Since 1983, the institutions have been working together to ensure their historical archives undergo uniform processing. The institutions have also established contact with national archive services and with several national archivists' associations whose role in the conservation and exploitation of archives should not be overlooked. Since archival documents relating to Community matters are held by the Member States as well as the institutions, there is plenty of opportunity for experimenting with new forms of synergy that could perhaps be extended to the whole of Europe's archival heritage.

9.1. THE 1983 DECISIONS

The Council Regulation and the Commission Decision of 1 and 8 February 1983[32] opened the historical archives of the ECSC (from January 1983) and of the EEC and Euratom (from January 1989) to the public in accordance with the 30-year rule. The political significance of the two texts lay in the 12 Member States and the Community institutions agreeing to act together for the first time in this sensitive new area and to pursue the same objectives, to follow certain agreed fundamental rules, and to develop new forms of cooperation.

9.2. BASIC OBJECTIVES AND PRINCIPLES

The opening of the Community's historical archives to the public had a threefold objective:

---

[32] Council Regulation (EEC, Euratom) No 354/83 and Commission Decision No 359/83/ECSC.

(a) to encourage research on the history of the Communities;

(b) to promote public interest in the development of the European Community;

(c) to make the functioning of the European institutions appear more transparent.

The two measures taken in February 1983 gave the Member States and the institutions a common legal base for the following fundamental principles: definition of Community archives; period before opening to the public; special rules for certain confidential or secret documents; declassification procedures; the problem of Community documents located in the archives of the Member States; access to Community documents by users; location of archives.

9.3. ARCHIVAL METHODS IN USE IN THE INSTITUTIONS

The institutions took the view that it would be appropriate for them to harmonize their archive services, to ensure that the Community's historical archives were processed in as uniform a manner as possible and to facilitate public access.

In a historical archives context, the main archival methods applied in principle in the institutions are as follows.

9.3.1. Transfer and review of documents

Records that no longer have any administrative value are sent to the historical archives by the Directorates-General and other services.

As a first step, the various identification and preliminary review operations are carried out strictly in accordance with the principle of provenance.

Files sent to the historical archives usually contain documents covering a variety of subjects and a relatively long period. They are analysed from the historical, legal and administrative points of view, sorted and divided according to subject, category, and the tasks and responsibilities of the originating services (always with reference to the historical context).

An effort is made to ensure that the review is carried out as early as possible in the administrative life cycle of records (manual or computer).

9.3.2. Research and consultation

The historical archive services of the institutions also prepare, with the help of computers (Archis database), finding aids for each archival deposit, such as circulation slips, basic lists, inventories by provenance and subject, and indexes.

The historical archive services also have other research tools available: biographical card indexes, chronological card indexes, specific card indexes for speeches, organization charts, orientation charts, catalogues of reference works, etc., which are already accessible to the public and which will be published at a later date.

9.3.3. Conservation problems

In the 1950s and 1960s in particular, the quality of the paper used both for originals and for copies was not always ideally suited to permanent conservation in archive repositories. The institutions are therefore examining various ways of restoration and conservation of documents and records.

In this context, progressive microfilming is a first step in the preliminary conservation of documents and records selected for the historical archives.

With regard to computer archives, studies are being undertaken into ways of looking after them to take account of their specific characteristics and allow full use to be made of them.

9.4. FLORENCE

Following the signing of a contract on 17 December 1984 between the EUIF and the Commission, on behalf of all the institutions, original records that have been made public are deposited at the Institute, where they may be consulted by anyone with a valid reason and who agrees to observe the rules for users.

The advantage of this location is that the EUIF is an interdisciplinary research institute covering, among other subjects, the history of European integration.

Since 1984, between 25 000 and 30 000 historical records have already been deposited with the Institute, a new batch being delivered each year in accordance with the 30-year rule. This figure is likely to grow quickly since it is not just the ECSC archives that have been opened to the public, but also those of the EEC and Euratom (although in the latter case a certain number of documents are subject to special confidentiality rules under the Treaty or under secondary legislation).

9.5. COOPERATION BETWEEN THE INSTITUTIONS AND THE MEMBER STATES

The institutions are in regular contact for the purpose of strengthening cooperation on subjects such as methodology, management and opening to the public.

This cooperation also extends to Member States, resulting in increased cooperation between them and the institutions.

Various activities have taken place since 1983, including a number of meetings organized between archivists from the Foreign Ministries of the 12 Member States and the institutions. One outcome of the meetings was the publication of a *Guide to the archives of the Ministries of Foreign Affairs of the Member States of the European Communities and of the European Political Cooperation*. This was produced by a mixed working group set up following a meeting in Brussels of the archive services concerned in March 1987.

Other measures are being considered, such as:

 (i) setting up training programmes and/or courses;

(ii) information exchanges;

(iii) a work and research programme which would lead to standardization in information technology.

There are in fact a very large number of areas in which work could and should be carried out in common.

Over the last 10 years, there has been increasing interlocking of the archives of the Member States and the institutions, resulting in more and more frequent exchanges of archival information between the national archive services of the Member States and the institutions.

The resolution of 14 November 1991 and the creation, by the Commission, of a group of national experts appointed by the Member States and those responsible for archives policy at national level, are the fruit of cooperation which, in accordance with the wish expressed by the Directors of national archive services when the Community archives were first opened to the public in 1983, is growing stronger all the time.

The institutions also maintain contacts with several national archivists' associations within the Community, as they recognize the importance of the role of these associations in safeguarding and exploiting the European archival heritage.

CHAPTER 10

THE COMMUNITY AND ARCHIVES IN EUROPE

The Community is not a rigid entity. Beginning from a nucleus of six, it has passed successfully to nine, then to 10, then to 12 Member States, not including the countries which are linked with it by Association Agreements.

In spite of the difficulties and present tribulations of its development, the dynamic of the opening is continuing. The Community is preparing for privileged relationships with most of the EFTA countries within the framework of the European Economic Area and has agreed to open membership negotiations with some of them.

The group of experts considers that paying attention to the situation of archives in some countries, particularly of Central and Eastern Europe, will contribute to the reinforcement of democracy throughout Europe.

Since the upheavals symbolized by the fall of the Berlin Wall in 1989, the Community has not only given economic aid to the countries of Central and Eastern Europe, but has also accepted the possibility of concluding specific Europe Agreements, which carry for their signatories the significance of adherence and proximity.

The European Council Meeting in Lisbon, on 26 and 27 June 1992, established the principle according to which any European country, as long as it is democratic, respects the rights of man and is ready to accept Community acts, may become part of the Community.

In such a context, any archival concern expressed on a Community level cannot remain indifferent to this movement. Moreover it is true that countries which are today on one side or another of Community boundaries have numerous pages of history in common.

The resolution of 14 November 1991 considers that 'European archival heritage provides an indispensable resource for writing the history of Europe or of a given nation'. On the basis of this affirmation, indispensable archival sources which are situated on the European continent outside the Community should not be neglected.

This awareness is even more important in that archives in the countries of Central and Eastern Europe are in general in a state of decay, owing to a lack of funds and qualified personnel.

Remaining within the sphere of the resolution, attention given to the state of archives in certain countries or furthering cooperation with regard to their use will also contribute to reinforcement of democracy throughout Europe.

There is nothing strange about such a step and it even has a significant precedent, namely when PHARE was credited with ECU 5 million destined to further the process of democratization in Central and Eastern Europe.[33]

Also to be pointed out is the intervention requested of the Commission which led, in the sphere of archives, to the signature of one of the rare positive agreements between the delegations of the former Yugoslavia concerning its problems of succession. This related specifically to the salvage of the threatened archives of Bosnia-Herzegovina.

Whilst acknowledging that means are not unlimited and that an order of priorities must be maintained, there can be no denying that the concept of common home applies unreservedly to the European archival heritage.

---

[33] The remarks to this budget item specified that the amount 'must enable financial and technical aid to be provided on a non-party basis, through parliamentary institutions, for general civic education and democratic principles to be stabilized and reinforced, in countries with close or developing links with the European Community. These funds are not intended for election campaigns, however'. (OJ L 26, 3.2.1992, p. 1221).

ANNEXES

Annex 1

REFERENCES TO THE LAWS AND REGULATIONS CONCERNING ACCESS TO ARCHIVES

GERMANY

Bundesarchiv

Gesetz über die Sicherung und Nutzung von Archivgut des Bundes (Bundesarchivgesetz — BArchG) of 6 January 1988 (BGBl. I, p. 62). This law has already been amended twice:

— under the terms of the law relating to the Treaty of 31 August 1990 between the German Federal Republic and the German Democratic Republic relative to the establishment of German unity (Unification Treaty) — Einigungsvertragsgesetz — of 23 September 1990 (BGBl. II, p. 885), Article 2, paragraph 8 has been extended to 'institutions of the German Democratic Republic';

— the law amending the BArchG of 13 March 1992 (BGBl. I, p. 506) enlarged the field of application of the latter to documents from the (political) parties and mass organizations of the German Democratic Republic which should be classified in the Federal archives under non-unilateral public law.

On the other hand, documents from the Ministry of State Security, the use of which is governed by the law relating to documents from the State security departments of the former German Democratic Republic (Stasi-Unterlagen-Gesetz — StUG) of 20 December 1991 (BGBl. I, p. 2272) are still not governed by the BArchG.

Länder

Baden-Württemberg: Law relating to the maintenance and use of archives (Landesarchivgesetz — LArchG) of 27 July 1987 (*Gesetzblatt für Baden-Württemberg, p. 230*), supplemented by the law relating to amendment of the Landesarchivgesetz of 12 March 1990 (Gesetzblatt für Baden-Württemberg, p. 89).

North Rhine-Westphalia: Law relating to the security and use of public archives in the *Land* of North Rhine-Westphalia (Archivgesetz Nordrhein-Westfalen — ArchivG NW) of 16 May 1989 (*Gesetz- und Verordnungsblatt für das Land Nordrhein-Westfalen*), p. 302).

Hesse: Hessisches Archivgesetz (HArchivG) of 18 October 1989 (*Gesetz- und Verordnungsblatt für das Land Hessen I*, p. 270).

Bavaria: Bayerisches Archivgesetz (BayArchG) of 22 December 1989 (KWMBl. I, p. 22).

Rhineland-Palatinate: Landesarchivgesetz (LArchG) of 5 October 1990 (*Gesetz- und Verordnungsblatt für das Land Rheinland-Pfalz*, p. 277).

Hamburg: Hamburgisches Archivgesetz (HmbArchG) of 21 January 1991 (*Hamburgisches Gesetz- und Verordnungsblatt I*, p. 7).

Bremen: Law relating to the security and use of public archives in the *Land* of Bremen (Bremisches Archivgesetz — BremArchG) of 7 May 1991 (*Gesetzblatt der Freien Hansestadt Bremen*, p. 159).

Thuringia: Law relating to the security and use of the archives (Thüringer Archivgesetz — ThürArchivG) of 24 April 1992 (*Gesetz- und Verordnungsblatt für das Land Thüringen, p. 137*).

Schleswig-Holstein: Law relating to the security and use of public archives in Schleswig-Holstein (Landesarchivgesetz — LArchG) of 11 August 1992 (*Gesetz- und Verordnungsblatt für Schleswig-Holstein*, p. 443).

Saarland: Saarländisches Archivgesetz (SArchG) of 23 September 1992 (*Amtsblatt des Saarlandes*, p. 1094).

BELGIUM

Loi relative aux archives, 24 juin 1955.

DENMARK

— Law on Public Archives, 14 May 1992.

— Order of 21 October 1992 concerning public archives.

SPAIN

— Constitución Española, articulo 105 B

— Ley de 8 de junio de 1957 sobre el Registro Civil

— Decreto de 14 de noviembre de 1958 por el que se aprueba del Reglamento del Registro Civil

— Ley de Secretos Oficiales de 1968

— Ley 48/1978 de 7 de octubre por la que se modifica la Ley de 5 de abril de 1968 sobre Secretos Oficiales

— Ley orgánica 1/1982 de 5 de mayo de protección civil del derecho al honor, a la intimidad personal y familiar y a la propria imagen

— Orden de 16 de enero de 1984 por la que se autoriza la consulta de documentos con fines de investigacion en el Archivo General y Biblioteca del Ministerio de Asuntos Exteriores

— Ley 16/1985 de Patrimonio Historico Español

— Real Decreto 111/1986 de desarrollo parcial de la ley 16/1985 de Patrimonio Historico Español

— Ley 14/1986 de 25 de abril General de Sanidad

— Ley 22/1987 de 11 de noviembre de Propriedad Intelectual

— Ley 12/1989 de 9 de mayo de la Funcion Estadistica Publica

— Ley 30/1992 de 26 de noviembre de Regimen Juridico de las Administraciones Publicas y del Procedimiento Administrativo Comun

FRANCE

— Loi 78-753 du 17 juillet 1978 sur la liberté d'accès aux documents administratifs

— Loi 79-18 du 3 janvier 1979 sur les archives

— Décrets des 3 décembre 1979 et 1er décembre 1980 pour l'application de la loi du 3 janvier 1979

GREECE

Law No 1946 on the General State Archives, May 1991

IRELAND

— National Archives Act 1986; Regulations 1988

— Official Secrets Act 1963

— Local Government Act 1994, section 65

ITALY

— DPR No 1409, 30 settembre 1963

— DPR No 854, 30 dicembre 1975

— Legge No. 241 of 7 agosto 1990 (diritto d'accesso ai documenti amministrativi)

LUXEMBOURG

— Arrêté grand-ducal du 21 octobre 1960 sur les Archives de l'État

— Loi du 28 décembre 1988 portant réorganisation des instituts culturels de l'État

NETHERLANDS

— Law on administrative openness (Wet Openbaarheid van Bestuur) of 1978, replaced by a new Law in 1991

— Archives Law (Archiefwet), 19 July 1962 (*Staatsblad* 313)

— Decision on Archives (Archiefsbesluit), 26 March 1968 (*Staatsblad* 200)

PORTUGAL

— Decreto 19952 of 27 de Junho de 1931

— Decreto-Lei 46350 of 22 de Maio de 1965

— Decreto-Lei N° 149/83, of 5 de Abril de 1983

— Decreto-Lei 106-G-92 of 1 de Junho de 1992

— Decreto-Lei N° 16/93 de 23 de Janeiro

UNITED KINGDOM

— Public Records Act (Northern Ireland) 1923

— Public Records (Scotland) Act 1937

— Public Records Act 1958

— Public Records Act 1967

— Official Secrets Act 1989

ARCHIVES ADVISORY COMMITTEES

BELGIUM

A Scientific Council on Archives has been in existence since 1970, composed of one half archivists and one half scientists. It has authority in particular with regard to access to archives less than 50 years old.

GREECE

In Greece, there is a Higher Archives Committee, of nine members.

SPAIN

The Consejo del Patrimonio Historico, as a collegiate body, is concerned with the application of the law on Spanish historic heritage. In Spain there is also a Comision Superior Calificadora de Documentos Administrativos and a Junta Superior de Archivos, which act as advisory bodies.

FRANCE

The Higher Archives Council (archivists, professors or members of universities or scientific institutions, genealogists), which was created on 21 January 1988, advises the Minister for Culture with regard to public and private archives. The Ministries of Justice and Finance have their own advisory committees.

IRELAND

The National Archives Advisory Council was set up in 1987 under the National Archives Act 1986. It advises the Minister for Arts, Culture and the Gaeltacht and the Taoiseach in the performance of their duties as laid down in the Act and in all matters relating to archives and their use by the public. The Council has 12 members, most of whom are historians or archivists not employed by the National Archives. The Director of the National Archives is not a member of the Council but is entitled to attend its meetings.

ITALY

Within the National Council for Cultural Goods and the Environment (an advisory body), which is presided over by the Minister and has 91 members, an advisory committee of nine members (Comitato di Settore Beni Archivistici) is responsible for archives. Sitting on this committee are three archivists, including the Director of the National Archives and administration representatives. Their advice is given on budgeting (particularly regarding the allocation of private donations), sorting and disposal, purchasing and depositing documents, etc.

NETHERLANDS

An Archives Council was created in 1968 to inform the Minister on questions related to the archives. Its prerogatives were taken over in 1990 by the State Archives Committee (Rijkscommissie voor de archieven) which is a part of the Council for Cultural Assets (Raad voor het cultuurbeheer). This is comprised of government representatives, archivists, record-managers and archive users. Its advice relates to review, conservation and access policies, legislation and regulations.

PORTUGAL

There is a Conselho consultivo composed of the director, the sub-directors, the director of the Archival and Inventory Services, two directors of the dependent archives designated by the Director of the AN/TT and also five individuals of known merit nominated by the member of government responsible for cultural matters.

UNITED KINGDOM

The Advisory Council on Public Records (ACPR) advises the Minister responsible, the Lord Chancellor, on the closure of records beyond the 30-year rule period and also principally on the public service of the National Archives, i.e. access to the archives, publications and prices for services offered. It has no executive role. It is chaired by the Master of the Rolls, and the secretariat is provided by the Lord Chancellor's Department. Its membership comprises the Keeper of the National Archives (PRO), senior civil servants on retirement, historians and archivists, and Members of Parliament.

The Scottish Records Advisory Council performs the same function in Scotland.

MONITORING OF RECORDS MANAGEMENT: APPRAISAL AND DISPOSAL BY THE NATIONAL ARCHIVES

Member States Respective roles of the government and the national archives.

BELGIUM

Archives held by the public authorities of the State, the provinces or by other public departments cannot be destroyed without prior authorization from the general archivist or his delegates.

DENMARK

Technical assistance from the National Archives to (central and local) authorities producing archives; review of definitive archives of the central and, where appropriate, municipal authorities by the National Archives. Any destruction must be authorized by the national archivist for central and municipal archives.

GERMANY (Bundesarchiv)

Preparation of schedules by the Bundesarchiv and responsibility of the latter at the time of sorting.

GERMANY (*Länder*)

Each *Land* lays down its own directives regarding review.

GREECE

The National Archives authorize the disposal of public archives.

SPAIN

A Comision Superior Calificadora de Documentos Administrativos was created by the law on Spanish historic heritage and given responsibility for evaluating archives. It is presided over by the Ministry of Culture and archive-producing authorities are represented. It prepares review tables. Notwithstanding this, the disposal of archives must be authorized by the Ministry of Culture. Each autonomous government can organize a committee of this kind.

FRANCE

Review schedules exist at all levels (State, region, *département*, local authority). The National Archives prepare lists of eliminable items and have scientific and technical control of review operations; the government authorizes the lists and carries out the review but if necessary the National Archives can carry out the review instead.

IRELAND

The archives of departments and Courts of Justice cannot be destroyed without the prior written approval of the Director of the National Archives.

ITALY

Mixed supervisory committees exist for each department of the government to provincial level, comprised of members of that department. They prepare lists of eliminable items and can require the deposit of archives threatened with destruction. The 20 superintendents responsible for inspecting the archives must approve decisions by the municipalities regarding the disposal of documents.

NETHERLANDS

The National Archives and the government prepare review schedules in collaboration. The State Archives Committee gives advice on each draft review schedule.

PORTUGAL

The review schedules are established by the National Archives and the administration. Each draft review schedule must be evaluated by the State Archives Committee.

UNITED KINGDOM

The departmental record officer undertakes a single review operation five years after the files are closed; when the archives are 25 years old a second review is carried out with the inspecting officer of the PRO.

Annex 4

EXTRACT FROM THE GERMAN CRIMINAL CODE
(PARAGRAPH 203) ON THE VIOLATION OF PRIVATE SECRETS

(Memorandum of 10 March 1987, finally amended by the Law of 9 June 1989; BGBl. 1871, p. 127; BGBl. I 1987, p. 945; correction p. 1160; BGBl. I 1989, p. 1059)

(1) Anyone whoever who divulges a secret which does not belong to him, namely a secret relating to someone's private life or a professional or commercial secret, which is given to him in his capacity as:

1. doctor, dentist, veterinary surgeon, pharmacist, or a member of other related professions, the pursuit of which or use of the title requires training which is given in accordance with public regulations,

2. professional psychologist having taken an examination at the end of a scientific apprenticeship recognized by the State.

3. lawyer, patent adviser, solicitor, defending lawyer in legal proceedings, economic or financial accounts expert, sworn accountant, tax adviser having fiscal power, or governing body or member of a governing body of an economic and financial accounts company, accounts company or taxation advice company,

4. matrimonial counsellor, education or young peoples' counsellor, counsellor on drug addiction, recognized by an authority or a body, institution or foundation under public law,

4a. member or representative of a guidance service recognized pursuant to Article 218b, paragraph 2, No 1,

5. member of a social service recognized by the State or an educational service recognized by the State, or

6. member of an illness, accident or non-occupational insurance company, or of a private medical compensation company,

is liable to punishment by imprisonment for a maximum of one year or by a fine.

(2) Also liable to prosecution is anyone whoever who divulges a secret not belonging to him, namely a secret relating to someone's private life or an industrial or professional secret which is given in his capacity as:

1. holder of a responsibility,

2. a public service executive,

3. a person assuming tasks and powers in accordance with legislation relating to the representation of personnel,

4. member of a committee of enquiry working for a legislative body of the Federal government or of a *Land*, of other committees or councils, who is not himself a member of the legislative or auxiliary body of such a committee or council,

5. an expert sent by the public authorities, formally engaged in scrupulously carrying out the obligations conferred upon him in accordance with a law.

In the sense of the first part, specific information relating to personal situation or objective details relating to another person, obtained with a view to carrying out public administrative tasks, are considered to be secret. The first part is not, however, applicable in so far as the specific information has been given to other authorities or other bodies with a view to the exercise of public administration if the law does not oppose this.

(3) Assistants and people working for the persons cited in paragraph 1 are considered in the same way as the latter in as much as they work with these persons as part of their professional training. Any person who comes into possession of a secret as a result of the death or succession of one of the persons cited in paragraph 1, first sentence, is bound by the same obligation of respect for secrecy.

(4) Paragraphs 1 to 3 are also applicable when a person divulges, without authorization, a secret which does not belong to him after the death of the person concerned.

(5) Any person acting for money or with the intention of enriching himself or a third party or of prejudicing a third party, is liable to a penalty of imprisonment for up to two years or a fine.

LAWS RELATING TO COMPUTER FILES

BELGIUM

Law relating to the protection of privacy with regard to processing data of a personal nature (1992).

DENMARK

Law No 654 of 20 September 1991. This stipulates that the competent authority with regard to inspection of computer files comes under the jurisdiction of a specific body, the Registertilsyn.

GERMANY

Datenschutzgesetz, 20 December 1990: Article 1 gives the law authority over archives with regard to modification, loss and inaccessibility of the files.

SPAIN

Computerized archives are protected by the Spanish Constitution of 1978 (Art. 18. 4°). Legislation is being prepared.

FRANCE

Law No 78-17 of 6 January 1978 relating to information technology, files and freedom. The National Committee on Computers and Liberty is responsible for inspecting computer applications handling personal information. The National Archives can appeal to this committee to obtain the deposit of files. By exception to the law on archives, files placed in the repositories of the National Archives are no longer available to the authorities who produced them.

IRELAND

Data Protection Act 1988.

LUXEMBOURG

Law of 31 March 1979 governing the use of personal data in computer processing.

NETHERLANDS

WPR (Wet persoonsregistratie), 8.9.1987, *Staatsblad* 665.

PORTUGAL

Constitution. Law No 1/89 of 8 July. Protection by Decree-Law 30/84 of 5 September 1984.

UNITED KINGDOM

Data Protection Act 1984.

Annex 6

REMOTE ACCESS TO ARCHIVAL INFORMATION IN THE SPANISH STATE ARCHIVES

1. At the CIDA (Centro de Información Documental de Archivos) various databases are being created (a census of archives, including over 30 000 archives; an archive bibliography, containing more than 10 000 references to professional publications; various guides to sources, such as that for the history of Italy, containing over 12 000 references, etc.).

These databases are accessible on-line as ASCII databases through the Ministry of Culture's central computer (which uses the Stairs information retrieval system, maintains its own network (PIC — cultural information points) and allows access to the switch telephone network), and through the Iberpac network, which follows the X.25 standard.

2. The Ministry of Culture has begun a videotext information service using the Ibertex network and in the near future a fair proportion of these databases will be accessible using this system.

3. The various State Archives will soon be able to link up with each other and with the Ministry of Culture, using the Iberpac network. The first consequence of this will be to give systematic access to the CIDA databases and to other cultural databases provided by the Ministry.

4. The second consequence of this link-up will be to allow the creation of a computerized archive network which will be based on the system developed by the Archivo General de Indias (the Indies Archives).

5. This system is expected to expand over the next few years (it is already being introduced into the National Historical Archives) and all the State Archives will eventually have the facilities to access information in other archives.

6. Although the main potential lies in accessing descriptive information in the rest of the archives, there are also other possibilities such as exchanging information between users. However, lines of communications currently only allow access to text, not pictures, because of the extra cost it would otherwise involve.

7. The possibility of disseminating this information through open networks will shortly be looked into. One possibility would be to convert the information, for its storage and dissemination, through the Ministry of Culture's present network although this would mean losing some of the advantages specifically developed for the Indies Archives system.

8. A direct link-up between the Indies Archives system and the future State Archives network is more complicated because the user would have to acquire the necessary hardware and software. An experiment is being carried out at the moment using a point-to-point line from the Huntingdon Library in Pasadena (California). With a user station similar to the one in Seville, it is possible to obtain on-line access to the textual database, and a copy of the digital images from various files in the Indies Archives which can be searched locally.

9. With regard to the possibility of applying CD-ROM to archival information, a CD-ROM containing black and white pictures (and colour for the Indies Archives) is currently being developed. This is a pilot project and the CD will be available from next July, others being planned to follow during the course of 1993-94.

Annex 7

LIST OF NATIONAL EXPERTS AND REPRESENTATIVES OF THE COMMUNITY INSTITUTIONS AND THE EUROPEAN UNIVERSITY INSTITUTE TAKING PART IN THE ARCHIVES PROJECT

(RESOLUTION OF 14 NOVEMBER 1991)

1. MEMBER STATES' EXPERTS

BELGIUM

Ernest Persoons
Archiviste Général
Archives Générales du Royaume
Rue de Ruysbroeck, 2
B-1000 Bruxelles
Tel. (32-2) 513 76 80
Fax (32-2) 513 76 81

Herman Coppens
Archives Générales du Royaume
Rue de Ruysbroeck, 2
B-1000 Bruxelles
Tel. (32-2) 513 76 80
Fax (32-2) 513 76 81

DENMARK

Johan Peter Noack
Rigsarkivar
Rigsdagsgarden, 9
DK-1218 København K
Tel. (45-33) 92 33 10
Fax (45-33) 15 32 39

Michael H. Gelting
Rigsarkivet
Rigsdagsgarden, 9
DK-1218 København K
Tel. (45-33) 92 33 10
Fax (45-33) 15 32 39

GERMANY

Prof. Dr Friedrich P. Kahlenberg
Präsident des Bundesarchivs
Potsdamer Straße 1
Postfach 320
D-56003 Koblenz
Tel. (49-261) 50 52 00
Fax (49-261) 50 52 26

Dr Hans Schmitz
Kultursministerium Nordrhein-
Westfalen
Völklinger Straße, 49
Postfach 101103
D-40002 Düsseldorf 1
Tel. (49-211) 896 03
Fax (49-211) 896 32 20

Dr. Hans-Joachim Schreckenbach
Ministerium für Wissenschaft,
Forschung und Kultur
Land Brandenburg
Friedrich-Ebert-Straße 4
Postfach 601162
D-14467 Potsdam
Tel. (49-331) 32 94 62
Fax (49-331) 276 36

GREECE

Marianna Kolyva
Directrice des Archives Générales
de l'État
Theatrou, 6
GR-10552 Athènes
Tel. (30-1) 32 19 601
Fax (30-1) 32 19 601

Nicolas Karapidakis
Chef-adjoint de division des archives
contemporaines
Theatrou, 6
GR-10552 Athènes
Tel. (30-1) 32 18 315
Fax (30-1) 32 18 315

SPAIN

Margarita Vazquez de Parga
Directora de los Archivos Estatales
Plaza del Rey, 1
E-28004 Madrid
Tel. (34-1) 521 56 26
Fax (34-1) 521 05 08

Pedro Gonzalez
Director del Archivo General de Indias
Avda. de la Constitucion, 3
E-41071 Sevilla
Tel. (34-95) 422 51 58
Fax (34-95) 421 94 95

FRANCE

Jean Favier
Directeur Général des Archives de
France
rue des Francs-Bourgeois, 60
F-75741 Paris Cedex 03
Tel. (33-1) 40 27 60 00
Fax (33-1) 40 27 66 01

François Renouard
Ministère des Affaires Étrangères
Directeur des Archives et de
la Documentation
Quai d'Orsay, 37
F-75342 Paris
Tel. (33-1) 47 53 42 53
Fax (33-1) 47 53 48 44

Michel Duchein
Inspecteur général honoraire
des Archives de France
118, av. Jean Jaurès
F-75942 Paris Cedex 19
Tel. (33-1) 42 03 22 87
Fax (33-1) 40 27 66 36

Paule Rene-Bazin
Direction des Archives de France
rue des Francs-Bourgeois, 60
F-75741 Paris Cedex 03
Tel. (33-1) 40 27 67 23
Fax (33-1) 40 27 66 47

Catherine Oudin
Ministère des Affaires Étrangères
Direction des Archives et de
la Documentation
Quai d'Orsay, 37
F-75342 Paris
Tel. (33-1) 47 53 53 53
Fax (33-1) 47 53 48 44

IRELAND

David V. Craig
Director of the National Archives
of Ireland
Bishop Street
Dublin 8
Tel. (353-1) 478 37 11
Fax (353-1) 478 36 50

Patrick Buckley
Executive Secretary, Royal Irish
Academy
Department of the Taoiseach
Government Buildings
Dublin 2
Tel. (353-1) 676 25 70
Fax (353-1) 676 23 46

ITALY

Renato Grispo
Capo di Gabinetto
Ministero per i Beni Culturali
e Ambientali
Via Gaeta, 8A
I-00185 Roma
Tel. (39-6) 494 14 64
Fax (39-6) 488 23 58

Salvatore Mastruzzi
Direttore generale per i beni archivistici
Ministero per i Beni Culturali
e Ambientali
Via Gaeta, 8A
I-00185 Roma
Tel. (39-6) 494 14 64
Fax (39-6) 488 23 58

M. Pia Rinaldi Mariani
Ufficio centrale per i beni archivistici
Ministero per i Beni Culturali
e Ambientali
Via Gaeta, 8A
I-00185 Roma
Tel. (39-6) 494 16 24
Fax (39-6) 487 22 23

Paola Tascini Stella
Ufficio centrale per i beni archivistici
Ministero per i Beni Culturali
e Ambientali
Via Gaeta, 8A
I-00185 Roma
Tel. (39-6) 494 16 24
Fax (39-6) 487 22 23

LUXEMBOURG

Cornel Meder
Archives nationales
BP 6
L-2010 Luxembourg
Tel. (352) 478 66 61
Fax (352) 47 46 92

NETHERLANDS

Eric Ketelaar
Algemeen Rijksarchivaris
Rijksarchiefdienst
Prins Willem Alexanderhof, 20
2500 EB Den Haag
Tel. (31-70) 331 55 50
Fax (31-70) 331 54 99

PORTUGAL

Jorge Borges de Macedo
Director do ANTT
Alameda da Universidade
P-1600 Lisboa
Tel. (351-1) 793 72 12/21
Fax (351-1) 793 72 30

Manuela Mendonca
ANTT
Alameda da Universidade
P-1600 Lisboa
Tel. (351-1) 793 72 12/21
Fax (351-1) 793 72 30

UNITED KINGDOM

Sarah Tyacke
Keeper of Public Records
Public Record Office
Kew, Richmond
Surrey TW9 4DU
Tel. (44-81) 878 12 50
Fax (44-81) 878 89 05

Patrick Cadell
Keeper of the Records of Scotland
HM General Register House
Edinburgh EH1 3YY
Tel. (44-31) 556 65 85
Fax (44-31) 557 95 69

2. EUIF REPRESENTATIVE

Jean-Marie Palayret
European University Institute
Piazza Edison, 11
Villa il Poggiolo
I-50133 Florence
Tel. (39-55) 468 56 26
Fax (39-55) 57 37 28

3. COMMISSION REPRESENTATIVES

Lino Facco
Chairman of the Group of Experts
Secretariat-General
Rue de la Loi, 200
Bur. Breydel 4/293
B-1049 Bruxelles
Tel. (32-2) 295 25 72
Fax (32-2) 296 59 66

Hans Hofmann
Secretary of the Group of Experts
Secretariat-General —
Historical archives
Rue de la Loi, 200
Bur. SDME — R1/70
B-1049 Bruxelles
Tel. (32-2) 295 20 53
Fax (32-2) 296 10 95

Jocelyne Collonval
Deputy secretary of the Group
of Experts
Secretariat-General —
Historical archives
Rue de la Loi, 200
Bur. SDME — R1/74
B-1049 Bruxelles
Tel. (32-2) 296 21 81
Fax (32-2) 296 10 95

Goetz Eike Zur Hausen
Legal Service
Rue de la Loi, 200
Bur. N-85 — 6/58
B-1049 Bruxelles
Tel. (32-2) 295 18 07/295 80 80
Fax (32-2) 295 24 93

Gerold Junior
Information technology directorate
Rue de la Loi, 200
Bur. IMCO 05/21
B-1049 Bruxelles
Tel. (32-2) 295 41 41
Fax (32-2) 295 50 75

Bénédicte Selfslagh
DG X — Culture unit
Rue de la Loi, 200
Bur. TR 120 — 4/46
B-1049 Bruxelles
Tel. (32-2) 299 92 48
Fax (32-2) 299 92 83

George Papapavlou
DG XIII/E/1
Bur. JMO B4/13
L-2920 Luxembourg
Tel. (352) 4301-343 18
     (352) 4301-329 63
Fax (352) 4301-328 47

Patricia MANSON
DG XIII/E/3
Librairies unit services
Bur. JMO C5-68
L-2920 Luxembourg
Tel. (352) 4301-332 61
Fax (352) 4301-321 69

René Brion
Commission expert
73 Berkendallaan
B-1800 Vilvoorde
Tel. (32-2) 267 25 53

Jean-Louis Moreau
Commission expert
92/6 avenue de Chérémont
B-1300 Wavre
Tel. (32-10) 24 11 10

4. REPRESENTATIVES OF OTHER INSTITUTIONS

Hartmut Berger
Central archives of the Council
Rue de la Loi, 170
B-1048 Bruxelles
Tel. (32-2) 294 73 05
Fax (32-2) 294 81 24

Jacques Schouller
European Parliament
Bâtiment Tour 125
L-2929 Luxembourg
Tel. (352) 43 00 32 72
     (352) 43 00 32 75
Fax (352) 43 94 93

Ian Hamilton
European Court of Auditors
Rue Alcide De Gasperi, 12
L-1615 Luxembourg
Tel. (352) 436 44
Fax (352) 43 93 42

Costantino Picco
Economic and Social Committee
3/312
Rue Ravenstein, 2
B-1000 Bruxelles
Tel. (32-2) 519 92 29
Fax (32-2) 513 48 93

5. OPOCE REPRESENTATIVE

John Young
Publications Office
Rue Mercier, 2
L-2985 Luxembourg
Tel. (352) 49928-42656
Fax (352) 48 88 57

LIST OF ABBREVIATIONS

AACR2	Anglo-American cataloguing rules (2nd edition)
ACCIS	Administration Committee for the Coordination of Information Systems
ACPR	Advisory Council on Public Records
ANTT	Arquivos Nacionais / Torre do Tombo — Portugal
ASCII	American Standard Code for Information Interchange
BArchG	Bundesarchivgesetz
CCITT	International Telegraph and Telephone Consultative Committee
CEN	Comité européen de normalisation (see ECS)
CIA	Conseil international des archives (see ICA)
CIDA	Centre de Información Documental de Archivos
CNIL	Commission nationale de l'informatique et des libertés — France
DLM	données lisibles par machine (see MRA)
DPR	Decreto del Presidente della Repubblica — Italy
DTAM	document transfer, access and manipulation
ECS	European Committee for Standardization (see CEN)
EDI	electronic document interchange
EDV	Elektronische Datenverarbeitung
FTAM	file transfer, access and manipulation
ICA	International Council on Archives (see CIA)
IRDS	information resources dictionary standard
ISDN	integrated services data network
ISO	International Organization for Standardization
MARC	machine-readable cataloguing
MIM	maquette d'interrogation multilingue/multilingual interrogation mock-up
MRA	machine-readable archives (see DLM)
ODA	office document architecture
ODIF	office document interchange format
OSI	open systems interconnection
PED	pôles économiques de développement
PIC	points d'information culturelle/cultural information points
PRO	Public Record Office
PSDN	packet switched data network
PSTN	public switched telephone network (see RTC)
RAMP	Records and Archives Management Programme
RLG	Research Library Group
RLIN	Research Librari Information Network
RTC	réseau téléphonique commuté (see PSTN)
SRO	Scottish Record Office
WPR	Wet persoonsregistratie — Netherlands

European Commission

Archives in the European Union

Luxembourg: Office for Official Publications of the European Communities

1994 — XVIII, 102 pp. — 17.6 x 25.0 cm

ISBN 92-826-8233-1

Price (excluding VAT) in Luxembourg: ECU 10